SOCIAL
MINISTRY

SOCIAL MINISTRY

An Urgent Agenda for Pastors and Churches

Haskell M. Miller

Foreword by J. Philip Wogaman

Herald
Press

Scottdale, Pennsylvania
Waterloo, Ontario

Library of Congress Cataloguing-in-Publication Data
Miller, Haskell M., 1910-
    Social Ministry: an urgent agenda for pastors and churches /
    Haskell M. Miller.
       p. cm.
    Includes bibliographical references.
    ISBN 0-8361-9138-2 (alk. paper)
      1. Church and social problems. 2. Sociology, Christian.
    3. Church work. I. Title.

BV625. M47 2000
261.8--dc21
                                      00-022506

All Bible quotations are used by permission, all rights reserved and
from *The Revised Standard Version of the Bible*, copyrighted 1946,
1952, 1971, 1973 by the Division of Christian Education of the
National Council of the Churches of Christ in the U.S.A.

SOCIAL MINISTRY
Copyright © 2000 by Herald Press, Scottdale, Pa. 15683
       Published simultaneously in Canada by Herald Press,
       Waterloo, Ont. N2L 6H7. All rights reserved
Library of Congress Catalog Number: 00-022506
International Standard Book Number: 0-8361-9138-2
Printed in the United States of America
Book design by Merrill R. Miller, Herald Press, in collaboration with
Michael A. King, Pandora Press U.S.
Cover design by Merrill R. Miller, Herald Press

10 09 08 07 06 05 04 03 02 01 00   10 9 8 7 6 5 4 3 2 1

To order or request information, please call
1-800-759-4447 (individuals); 1-800-245-7894 (trade).
Website: www.mph.org

*To
all the students
I have hoped to
impress with these points.*

Contents

Foreword

first became acquainted with Haskell Miller in a 1961 conference on Christian social concerns. He had become Professor of Sociology and Social Ethics at Wesley Theological Seminary in Washington, D.C. He was at the same time a part-time research director for the national Methodist social concerns agency, also located in the nation's capital. I thought that was a splendid combination of responsibilities, and I was impressed what Dr. Miller had to say at the conference. Little did I realize that we would become colleagues on the Wesley faculty five years later.

During the ten years we worked together, we team-taught the seminary's introductory course in Christian ethics and shared in a variety of projects. He impressed me. Here he was, a sociologist, and a good one. But he was also passionately alive to social problems and on fire with the conviction that every pastor sent out from the seminary should be an intelligent moral leader. Don't be misled by his comment in this book that he is a social scientist and not a theologian! It is possible to be both. More's the pity that so few theologians have paid attention to insights from the social sciences.

This book demonstrates how Miller has remained alive to his vocation of teaching. *Social Ministry* is easily read and is eminently practical, as Miller challenges pastors to get beyond the superficial. Here and there throughout one runs into passages like this one:

> Give attention to your homiletical style. Will you stick uncritically to the Bible text, as though God has slept and nothing has changed since it was written? Will you be

dully conventional, massaging individual psyches with reminders of God's grace and promises of eternal salvation? Will you emphasize histrionics and entertainment, coated with a veneer of biblical piety? Or will you do your best to be interesting, relevant to realities in society and to what people are experiencing, and firmly grounded in your best theological understandings of the spirit and message of the Bible? If you are convinced of the biblical mandate for, and validity of, social action as a part of your ministry, your preaching will necessarily have a prophetic tone.

Amen to that!

This book is not long enough for detailed commentary on all the theological and social issues it raises, nor is that its purpose. No doubt every reader will find points of agreement and disagreement. But any thoughtful reader will be driven to self-examination of his or her ministry and to further study and action.

In addition to the immense theological diversity of North American churches, I am impressed by the great differences of size, cultural context, and practical opportunities for service. But a point this book underscores implicitly on every page is that every church has opportunities. No church should consider itself a backwater place of no significance. Every church is at some cutting edge of unique possibilities.

It is a great, God-given privilege to engage in ministry anywhere. I pray that many who read *Social Ministry* will find themselves re-energized by it.

—*J. Philip Wogaman, Senior Minister*
Foundry United Methodist Church
Washington, D.C.

Author's Preface

Social Ministry is a response to needs I felt during a long ministry, about half of which was in the pastorate and half in church college, university, and theological seminary teaching. As a pastor, I seemed almost constantly confronted with social problems and issues. I felt some obligation to respond to them but also felt uncertain and ill equipped. In teaching, especially where young seminarians were concerned, I became keenly aware of how little was being done to help students develop social awareness and to help prepare them for the responsibilities of leadership in dealing with social issues, handling social problems, and making major decisions affecting the quality of life in their communities.

Initially, I entered the ministry with an intuitive sense that the Christian religion related to the whole of life, that Christ came to save "the world" as well as lost individuals in it. The prayer for the kingdom's coming "on earth as it is in heaven" (Matt. 6:10) seemed highly meaningful and important to me.

My first full-time pastorate gave me an intense introduction to the social dimensions of ministry. Fresh out of Southern Methodist University, I found myself trying to be the pastor of a newly reorganized congregation in the heart of a booming oil field.

The field had recently been discovered in an impoverished, rural area of East Texas. The volume of people who had swarmed into this area had almost completely overwhelmed all of the forms of established, organized community life. The community was trying to re-form itself around the church and the public school. I found myself almost overwhelmed by social problems that had a direct and obvious relationship to my ministry.

In addition to what I learned through the challenges of practical experience, my graduate study in the social sciences, particularly in sociology, vastly expanded my understanding of social ministry. I gained insights into what it should include and what it could mean.

Over the years, I have tried to share what I have learned. The effort has always been handicapped, however, by a dearth of helpful literature on the subject. Important as it is, and is increasingly becoming, social ministry simply has not received the attention it should command.

A limited number of books have dealt in some way with the societal responsibilities of ministry. Many of these writings, however, have been specialized in approach: the church's social ministry, social ministry in theological education, community ministry, social action in pastoral counseling, and so on.

This book is intended to reflect broadly on the societal dimensions of ministry, and on social problems and ways of dealing with them as a Christian minister. I propose to address the pastor directly, making the best suggestions I can concerning social action as pastoral responsibility.

If at least a few pastors find the suggestions helpful, I shall be pleased. If in some small way the suggestions contribute to a more wholistic understanding of the gospel and its relevance to all of life, it will be an answer to prayer—mine, as well as the one Jesus taught us to pray.

—*Haskell M. Miller*
  Seaford, Delaware

Introduction

This book is meant primarily for pastors of North American Protestant or Anabaptist churches. Typically the Protestant pastor in the United States or Canada is employed by a congregation to perform a fairly standardized set of functions. She or he is usually selected, with or without denominational help, from a pool of those certified by the denomination to be qualified for the position. Members' offerings pay the pastor's salary, and the congregation looks to the pastor for overall leadership of its activities.

Often the pastor has significant freedom to develop his or her own job description. Within the bounds of a few loosely defined expectations, the position can be organized to fit the inclinations of the individual.

Social ministry generally has not been emphasized as an integral part of pastoral tradition. Thus, many pastors have been relatively unaware of this dimension of their responsibility. Others have found it convenient and expedient to disregard it.

In either case, social ministry has often been limited to dispensing tokens of paternalistic aid. Few pastors have been committed to passionate advocacy of social change to improve the lot of the needy or correct conditions of injustice.

Gradually, however, the situation is changing. More and more people entering the ministry have become socially aware through their educational backgrounds, the mass media, or personal experience.

These individuals are bringing to the pastoral ministry a more comprehensive, wholistic understanding of how the gospel relates to conditions of community life. They are eager to interpret the good news and see it implemented in all its fullness and redemptive power. Unfortunately, such people are still a minority, and their enthusiasm often takes them far ahead of the conservative, traditional positions the laity of their congregations are still anchored to.

This gap causes much of the misunderstanding between pastors and congregations that is currently disturbing nearly all denominations. It is indicative of the great need for pastors to become involved in their parishioners' continuing education.

The debate over social activism is not new. The conflict between so-called "fundamentalism" and "modernism" led to extremes in attitudes and emphases during the last half of the nineteenth century and early decades of the twentieth.

There were many reasons for the conflict. American culture on the whole was undergoing far-reaching change. The full impact of the newly developing scientific era was being felt, and the social sciences in particular were becoming a major influence.

The impact on theological thought was great. Science was developing views of physical and social reality that did not coincide with traditional biblical understandings.

Conservative impulses prompted many people to cling to what had been meaningful and valuable to them in the past. Other people became excited over the significance of the new insights.

Walter Rauschenbusch, a Baptist minister in New York City, helped to crystallize thought in church circles regarding the new developments. His speaking and writing in the early decades of the twentieth century launched what came to be known as the Social Gospel Movement.[1]

Rauschenbusch was impressed by the relevance of the gospel to the many trying conditions in modern society.

Informed by perspectives from science, he became keenly aware of neglected dimensions of Christian leadership. His emphasis on the social application of the gospel was in accord with the growing sentiments of many church people.

Others in the church strongly resisted Rauschenbusch's approach. Fundamentalism hardened its defenses of biblical perspectives to the point of irrationality and bibliolatry. Some social gospel advocates, meanwhile, drifted carelessly into superficial humanism and easy optimism concerning the inevitability of progress.

In recent decades, the extreme limits of each of these positions have been considerably modified. Though the chasm of difference still exists, each has assumed a more sober attitude toward Christian social activism.

Advocates of the social gospel tradition are grounding their thought and action in a more disciplined theology, especially in a Christology that is more realistic about human nature, sin, and social progress. Fundamentalism, in its own fashion, has embraced many biblical attitudes toward social sin and combined them with social conservatism to justify a dramatic and pragmatic form of social action. One form of such action has been the organized movement sometimes known as the Christian Right.

This means that responsibility for social action falls on the shoulders of pastors in both camps. Objectives and methods vary, but the skills needed and pressures faced are much the same. As the publication *Religion in the News* observed in its inaugural issue, "Today places of worship, regardless of creed, have become platforms for an astonishing range of educational and social services."[2]

SOCIAL MINISTRY

Chapter 1

The Pastoral Role

The Pastor

"So, you are a pastor. Why?"

This provocative question needs to be dealt with honestly. Your answer will have a major effect on your performance in the role you have assumed.

It is usually understood, of course, that you have had some special awareness of God, the great transcendent reality, from which you have felt called to preach the gospel. If, like the farmer of a humorous story, you had a vision of the letters G, P, and C flashed across the sky, you were sure it did not mean Go Plow Corn, or Go Punch Computers, but Go Preach Christ.

According to the *Encyclopedia Britannica*, a preacher is someone who believes that he or she is "the ambassador of God, charged with a message," and it is his or her duty to deliver.[3] This special personal sense of mission, regardless of how it was acquired, is all-important. It is what will fortify you for the pressures and difficulties you will experience in the pastorate. If you do not have a deeply ingrained sense of calling and mission, you are probably in the wrong profession.

It is not likely that you became a pastor because of the salary you expected to receive. The pay is not that good, though it is much better now than it has been—especially when Paul needed to make tents for a living.

If you entered pastoral ministry because of the prestige you thought the position would provide, you could be in for a surprise. The profession is steadily declining in status in the eyes of the populace.

It is more likely that you are a pastor because you felt a deep desire to become one. After sensing your calling, you probably spent much time and effort preparing for the role. Now your ambition is being realized.

At the same time, you are a pastor because a congregation has agreed to have you as its leader. The people of your church expect you to be their spiritual leader, but you will have to be much more than that. They expect also that you will lead them in the many tasks that the church program involves.

Actually, in many respects your position is much like that of the CEO of a corporation. You are the key person. Under your administrative leadership, the church program will flourish, decline, or remain static. Its activities and resources, while not totally under your control, will inevitably be influenced in the direction of your interests and inclinations. Remember, Paul addressed one of his churches as people "incorporate in Christ."

In view of the importance of your position, it is terribly important that you understand yourself.

You are fortunate if you have had the benefit of counseling based on a psychological analysis or personality inventory. In any case, you need to be aware of who you are and where you are coming from. The more you understand your makeup and style of functioning, the better you will be able to interpret the reactions of other people to you.

Are you conservative, liberal, middle-of-the-road, or with no identifiable philosophical identity? Are you a creative leader or a follower? Are you aggressive or shy and timid? Do you tend to feel inferior or superior to other people? Do you tend to speak and act deliberately, after careful thought, or are you inclined to react rapidly, often without sufficient thought beforehand? Do you have a lively imagination? Are you a priestly or a prophetic type?

All of these traits can make a great difference in your ministry. The admonition to know thyself, therefore, is quite important.

As a pastor, however, the bottom line is that you have the great privilege and satisfaction of preaching the gospel of God's love in Christ Jesus. You have the joyful opportunity to help people grow in Christ-like grace. You are the chief liturgist when your people worship the God of their faith, and you participate in ceremonies that mark the most important moments of their lives. All of these factors, and many other unexpected blessings, can make being a pastor a very rewarding experience.

The Pastoral Role

What do you consider your primary role as a pastor? Are you an evangelist, seeking to save souls? Are you a preacher, proclaiming the word of God to all who will listen? Are you the shepherd of a flock? Are you the inspirer, educator, and trainer of missionaries for their tasks in the world? Are you an entrepreneur, an administrator, or the caretaker of a nursery?

One such image, whether or not consciously acknowledged, will likely guide and dominate your performance. Yet at times you may feel you must fill all these roles and more.

A weary pastor with many years experience remarked that getting to preach the Word of God seemed a secondary part of his job. Most of his time and energy went to hatching, matching, patching, and dispatching. By this he meant christening infants, officiating at weddings, counseling the sick and distraught, and performing funerals.

These are a necessary part of being a pastor, and you will be blessed if you can see them as a vital and meaningful part of the privilege of the position. They are, however, peripheral to the central purpose of your ministry.

As noted previously, the pastoral role is diverse and complex. Its complexity has seemed to correlate rather closely with the increasing institutionalization of the church and the growing complexity of modern culture.

You will find that one of your biggest problems is that of covering all your bases and keeping a proper balance in what you do with your time and energy. Some pastors lose control and become overwhelmed.

This need not happen to you. Your best safeguards against exhaustion and burnout are—

- keeping your prayer life active and vital;
- maintaining sensitive awareness of why you are in the ministry;
- having a clear set of goals and objectives that are realistic in your context;
- having the courage and faith to commit yourself energetically to the pursuit of the goals and objectives you have set for yourself;
- maintaining faith that God is with you and that his grace is always all-sufficient for you; and carefully budgeting your time and energy.

Its difficulties notwithstanding, the pastoral role is one of the most privileged and rewarding of all human occupations. You need to keep this always uppermost in your thinking. Being a pastor comforts you with the assurance of being in a special partnership with God. It provides you with friends and a task of significance. It puts you in charge of an organization specifically designed for the purpose of inspiring, nurturing, and saving people—a unit of the body of Christ. It makes you the leader with social power and influence.

The Social Responsibility of the Role

Social action is a necessary part of your pastoral responsibility. It is neither optional nor avoidable. Everything you do as a pastor has social implications.

You are in charge of a congregation of people who have committed themselves to take up their crosses and follow Jesus. Hazards to their physical and spiritual welfare, however, grow more numerous every day, and they will need your help to find the ways of discipleship most needed in today's lost world.

As a pastor, therefore, you have social responsibilities beyond those of the lay person. You are an actor in the dynamic drama of community life. You are assigned a part; the only option you have is how you will play it. Will yours be a covert, overt, or inert performance?

The director of an urban ministry internship program observes that the only choice pastors have about the sociological aspects of ministry is what kind of agents they will be: insightful and effective, ignorant and prejudiced, or in default and ineffective. "You cannot take good care of persons," he declares, "without doing something about the environment which makes them what they are."[4]

You and your church have social responsibilities that cannot be avoided, though they may be denied. Not to recognize and assume those responsibilities, however, is a most significant form of action. The quality of response when the responsibility is recognized and assumed is what needs attention.

Chapter 2

The Christian and Justice

Justice is the minimum requirement of Christian love.

Problems of justice are represented in the many aspects of society where values are dispensed. Justice is at issue when laws are being drawn or enforced, when economic goods are being distributed, and when favors are being shown.

Love prescribes fairness. Alienation, however, produces much unfairness, and the church must not be indifferent to this, wherever it exists. The poor are often alienated and become victims of injustice, hard hearts, and lack of compassion. In the human pecking order, they are the ones for whom God has special concern.

The plight of the poor is a major tragedy and scandal of our time. It must be burned deeply in your heart as a pastor and impressed as fully as possible on the people of the congregations you serve.

The injustice that creates poverty was undoubtedly what Walter Rauschenbusch had in mind when he wrote that it is "the will and power of God to redeem the permanent institutions of human society from their inherited guilt of oppression and extortion."[5] It was what Karl Marx had in mind when he wrote *The Communist Manifesto*. It was what inspired liberation theology in Latin America.

The Bible expresses an incessant and unequivocal concern for the poor. Moses on Mount Sinai received instruction that fields should lie fallow each seventh year "that the poor of your people may eat" from them (Exod. 23:11). Amos prophesied against those that "trample the head of the poor into the dust of the earth" (Amos 2:7). The author of Proverbs declared: "The righteous know the rights of the poor; the wicked have no such knowledge" (Prov. 29:7).

Jesus said, "Blessed are you who are poor, for yours is the kingdom of God" (Luke 6:20). Moreover, he cited the fact that "the poor have good news preached to them" as proof of the authenticity of his ministry (Matt. 11:5).

These references provide only a few examples of the Bible's sentiments. Cruden's concordance lists 197 references to the poor.

The God we see in the Bible is deeply concerned about the plight of the poor. Can we doubt that God expects Christians and the church to be concerned also?

Poverty not only causes deprivation and suffering, it humiliates and degrades. Moreover, it evokes a sinful pride in successful people who dwell in its presence behind their barricades of power.

There are far more people in the world who are poor than there are who are comfortably middle class or prosperous. Hopefully, humanity will one day mature sufficiently to use the available technology to remedy this situation. The problem is not a matter of scarcity, but rather a difficulty of the mind and heart, of purpose and will.

This, the church must recognize, is where the gospel is focused. The gospel seeks a change of spirit, which through the power and grace of God prompts humanity to care more lovingly and adequately for all of its members.

Annual per capita income in the richest nation on earth is more than five hundred times that of the poorest nation. For example, the *Universal Almanac 1997* reported these 1995 hourly earnings (in U.S. dollars) for production workers: Belgium $26.88; Austria $25.38; Japan $23.66; U.S. $17.20; Greece $8.95; Mexico $1.51; and Sri Lanka $0.45. (These figures include wages, premiums, bonuses, vacation, holidays and other leave, insurance, and benefit plans.)

Figures for per capita Gross Domestic Product (GDP) show a similar picture, even when the numbers are adjusted for differences in the cost of living. According to the *1999 Time Almanac*, the adjusted GDP for the United States is $28,600 and Japan's is $22,700, compared to $1,000 for Haiti and only $430 for Ethiopia.

Average incomes, of course, conceal the disparities within each nation. All around the world, the position of the rich stands in sharp contrast to that of the poor.

In the United States, the contrast is indeed great. The highest incomes are astronomical, while some fifteen percent of the population lives below the poverty level. Many others, the working poor, manage their existence barely above the poverty level.

Can you imagine what it is like not to be able to afford the food for a balanced diet? Or to buy decent clothes for your children? Or to have adequate health insurance? Not only are such simple and basic amenities beyond the reach of hundreds of thousands of people in our society, they are associated with many other deprivations such as decent housing, reliable means of transportation, medical care, and many other things more prosperous people take for granted.

Poverty is not only deprivation; for most of the poor it is hopelessness. Because they see no chance of improving their lot, many become demoralized and sink into irresponsibility. When this occurs, it gives those with superior advantages an excuse for alienation. It enables them to make judgments and feel justified in the neglect that produced the demoralization.

With such attitudes, the relatively prosperous and rich can withdraw without guilt feelings. They can provide minimum crumbs of humiliating paternalism, and leave the poor to sweat out existence the best way they can, which is usually in neglected slums, where they gravitate out of helplessness.

Successful, prosperous, middle-class people withdraw from the poor to live in suburbs or special housing projects . There they enjoy a privileged social life as far from the sight of poverty as possible. The wealthy tend to be so imbued with class consciousness that they live behind walls, gates, and guards, as insulated as possible from all other social classes.

There are exceptions, of course, to this general picture. It tends, however, to be an accurate portrayal of the overall situation in our society and it is an assessment for you and the churches you serve to ponder. Is it a representation of Christian love, or of estrangement and alienation?

The poor are penalized in many ways. Money is power, and the only self-respecting means they have of obtaining money is through selling their time and labor. As a consequence, because they cannot do anything else, they get most of society's hardest and dirtiest jobs. People who have escaped from poverty define their escape in terms of relief from these jobs. They disparage them because the jobs are unpleasant and difficult.

If the poor had the power to reject them as others do, these jobs would quickly become some of the highest paid in society. The plight of the poor, therefore, is explained in terms of powerlessness, discrimination, and absence of the love Jesus spoke about.

The penalizing process finds expression in many other ways also. Where sales taxes exist, the poor pay a larger proportion of their income in taxes than do other people. The usual excuse given by the more prosperous for this disparity is that it is a way for the poor to "pay their share." This excuse, however, does not take into consideration the fact that the poor have had no opportunity to get their fair share in the first place.

Even in the courts, justice is not evenly dispensed. The poor are more heavily penalized, primarily because they do not have the money to pay expensive lawyers to defend them.

If they take refuge in the welfare system, they are subjected to many forms of humiliation. In fact, the welfare system is being operated so reluctantly and negatively that it is being accused of being punitive.

It would be easy for you to conduct your ministry without getting disturbed about the poor. They are so many, and so frequently in our presence that we fail to take notice of them. They are just a part of the landscape.

The story goes that a few years ago some members of a national church council made a house-to-house study of poverty in a southern state. At a meeting of church leaders, they gave a graphic report of their findings along a certain stretch of highway. A bishop in the audience took exception to their description of their findings. "I travel that road at least once or twice a week," he said, "and I've never seen anything like that!"

"But, Bishop," a member of the committee replied, "have you ever stopped to look?"

Stopping to look and trying to understand makes the difference. Do not take comfort in Jesus' observation that "you always have the poor with you" (Matt. 26:11). He was not approving or accepting poverty. He was saying that its existence should not be used as an excuse for neglecting to worship.

You and your congregation cannot solve the problem of poverty, but by the grace of God you can make a dent in it. You can be part of the solution. You can teach understanding and fairness. You can pay and demand decent wages. You can vote for economic policies that express ethical concern for the interests of all parties involved. You can stay aware and oppose unfair employment practices, wages, or discriminatory treatment of any kind.

You can reject social class attitudes and cultivate attitudes of compassion and caring. Wherever possible, you can help poor people help themselves. You can stay on guard against paternalism and seek ways of actively identifying with those who need your help. In short, you can be, and ought to be, advocates for the poor.

Chapter 3

The Pastor's Social Responsibility

As faith-inspired people bound together by the spirit of love and compassion expressed by Jesus, your local congregation provides a wonderful setting for redemptive social action. There are many modes of social action and ways you can undertake such action. You will need to discern, prayerfully and carefully, what your situation demands.

What Is Involved

An excellent outline of what socially responsible pastoral ministry involves is found in the report of a seminar held at Wesley Theological Seminary in Washington, D. C. in l987.

Papers presented by twenty-three participants from six major denominations were summarized by one of the participants and are presented here. You should give serious attention to each of these items:

1. Socially Responsible Ministry (SRM) involves a 'radical critique' of society, depending in part on careful listening to the oppressed. It is lived Christian practice that 'envisions the whole,' placing ministry in the context of large social trends.

2. There is no neutral ministry. All ministry is socially responsive in some way. The question is how. SRM is a liberating ministry that emerges concretely out of the oppressed community.

3. SRM requires social analysis and consciousness of the ethos we live in. It demands personal, institutional, and ecclesial self critique. It is not the same as focusing on social issues.

4. SRM features praxis or struggle for liberation of the oppressed. It requires critical awareness of the tendencies that derive from our own social location. It needs memory and vision—past and future.

5. SRM follows the logic of *missio dei,* the mission of God, in its wholeness, and participates in the unified mission of the church. It develops as Christians shaped by the Christian story, become worshipping and witnessing people who have theological discipline and are socio-culturally aware.

6. SRM is oriented to doing justice, making peace, and caring for creation. It requires walking with the oppressed in shared ministry and in working for social policy change. It affirms the communal nature of human existence and is expressed in all basic functions of the church.

7. SRM requires "solidarity"—loyalty to disregarded people, not ideological causes. It is rooted in spirituality and love, guided by the vision of shalom. It requires critical analysis and institutional reform. [6]

Focus of Concern

You should be concerned with both the local community and the larger community that lies beyond. Conditions requiring your attention and that of your church may exist, or develop suddenly, in either.

Many aspects of community life will require your continuous attention, including the following:

- human welfare needs and the adequacy of provisions for meeting those needs;
- environmental protection and preservation;
- inequities and injustices that cause needless suffering;
- the treatment of social offenders;
- influence of the media and mass communication;
- conditions affecting family life;
- uses and abuses of political power;
- conflict;
- prejudice and alienation.

In addition to community issues, there are national and world issues such as war, production and distribution of weapons (especially nuclear weapons), hunger, population control, trade relations, and the like.

For most of these matters, the need and practical opportunity for action may never arise. If and when they do, however, you and your congregation should be aware of it and be ready to follow the Holy Spirit's leadership.

An Objective of Change

In all of these areas cited, it is implied that change is needed. Something is wrong and action is required to try to set it right. Prayerful Christian action is an effort to bring an evil under the judgment and redeeming grace of God. In this regard, social ministry is much like the evangelism that seeks the salvation of lost souls.

It seems safe to assume that God is opposed to evil wherever it exists. Thus when evil enters social institutions and other organized aspects of society, which it does often, these social structures need to be changed, redeemed.

Appropriate Attitudes

Considered in this light, Christian social action must be thought of as an effort in keeping with our understanding of God's will. Because it is God's work, it should always be accompanied by much prayer and care. It should be Christ-centered and firmly anchored in God's love and grace.

Because social action is based on personal opinion of God's will, it should be held tentatively. One should always be open to further revelation. Action should always flow from full faith commitment, but we must also remember that human judgment is subject to error. We can learn from mistakes, especially when they are sincerely made.

We also must remember that all humans are God's children. People opposing the action you and your congregation are involved in, no matter how difficult they are or how much a part of the problem they may be, are also subjects of God's love, and should be viewed and treated as such.

Seeing the Community as a Whole

It is also important that you see your community as a whole, as a functional entity with its own unique features. You will need to recognize the many facets of your community and the ways that it is connected with the larger region, the nation, and the world.

John Wesley, preaching on London streets, saw the world as his parish. Your ministry will be tragically small if you restrict it and your vision to the walls or program boundaries of your church. You need to be aware of the unique features of your community, as well as of your congregation, and relate your ministry to them as fully as possible.

Injunctions and Admonitions

So important is your ministry of redemptive social action that there are many admonitions and injunctions that clamor for your attention, whether you are just beginning your career or are several years into it. Among them are the following:

1. *Stay focused on God's love, grace, and intentional will.* If you lose sight of these anchor points, the value of your efforts will be greatly limited.

2. *Beware of the Lone Ranger syndrome.* Don't try to do it all yourself; get all the help you can. Cooperate with other people, agencies, or programs wherever possible. Don't seek for your church to be the star performer.

Sometimes your congregation may have to function alone or in positions of prominence; make sure this is the result of a natural course of events, not the outgrowth of pride, arrogant exclusiveness, or simple self-centeredness.

3. *Be prepared.* Be sure to have the facts straight and know what you are talking about. Marshal your resources.

4. *Stay alert.* Keep your eyes and ears open and weigh your options. Don't start something you aren't prepared to finish, or are at least resolved to give your best effort.

5. *Avoid trivialities.* There are so many important things to be concerned about that it is a shame to waste effort on things that matter little. As the saying goes, "Don't strain at a gnat and swallow a camel."

6. *Accept unavoidable controversy.* Since social action usually seeks needed change, opposition is unavoidable. Controversy, therefore, is to be expected. Avoid it where possible, but do not be afraid of it. When you must engage in it, remember to maintain such dignity and spirit as becomes a follower of Jesus. There is more than a germ of truth in the old saying that your job is to comfort the afflicted and afflict the comfortable. You will find this difficult to do without stirring things up a bit.

Martin Luther King Jr. addressed this issue succinctly in his *Letters from a Birmingham Jail.* "The great stumbling block," he said, "is the moderate Christian who prefers a negative peace, which is the absence of tension, to a positive peace, which is the presence of justice."[7]

7. *Seek ways to accentuate the positive.* The best kind of social action provides for meeting needs before bad arrangements are structured. An ounce of prevention is always worth more than a pound of cure.

8. *Keep your halo on straight.* Don't allow self-centered pride to corrupt your efforts. Be sincere in your concerns. Be dedicated. Be humble.

9. *Discipline yourself.* Be consistent. Practice what you preach. In the long run, you'll have to win confidence, support, and the right to be heard.

10. *Keep the flower of commitment watered and bright.* Remember who you are, and whose you are. No one should tackle "the powers of this world" without putting on daily "the whole armor of God." Prayer, study (especially of the Bible), and renewal of commitment are indispensable.

Conclusion

Your social ministry responsibility is great and involves preventive as well as corrective effort. It begins with the local church and community and extends to the world. It involves alertness, thoughtfulness, caring, and courage, anchored in Scripture and faith.

Social action is a vital part of your ministry, inseparable from the responsibility to preach the word of God's redeeming love so wonderfully revealed in Jesus Christ. It is a major dimension of the most important work in the world.

Your immediate and direct social action responsibility comes down to two key tasks. First, you need to help your lay people equip themselves for their responsibilities as lay ministers in society. Second, you must guide the church in developing and operating its program of social ministry.

The author of a report on a major church and community project that involved many volunteers and twenty-five churches, said the volunteers credited their pastors with contributing to their growth through the projects in two primary ways: by encouraging them individually to become involved in the projects, and by preaching from the pulpit a linkage between faith and social ministry.[8]

A point should be added, also, about trusting the people of your congregation. They have made commitments to Christ and may be better prepared than you think to respond to challenges that require expression of their faith. The author of the report mentioned above said that "pastors consistently and significantly underestimated congregational support for community ministry."[9]

Pastors, it seems, were more comfortable with and attracted to pastoral nurture. They feared potential conflicts that could develop in community ministries. Half of the pastors initially contacted about participating in the project expressed this fear. A fourth of them rejected participation, saying, "My members would not support it."[10]

Chapter 4

Difficulties to Be Anticipated

Socially relevant action may be the most difficult part of your ministry. It has been seriously neglected by tradition and made controversial in recent church history. Understanding its importance rests heavily on insights brought to light since the advent of the social sciences. The church is just beginning to accept the concept as a legitimate part of its ministry. Many difficulties can be anticipated. The following sections discuss some of the major ones.

Your Limited Education

Unfortunately, your seminary education probably did not give you much guidance on how to recognize and initiate socially relevant action. Chances are that you never had a course on, or serious mention of, the subject.

Most seminaries are just beginning to be aware of the need for instruction in addressing this topic. Consequently, you will have to devote yourself to the development of skills on your own. You can do this by reading everything relevant you can find, by conferring with pastors who have had experience in the matter, and by paying thoughtful attention to learning by doing.

The Limitations of Tradition

Christian tradition is quite limited when it comes to socially relevant action. Relationships to people on the basis of compassion and love developed easily and naturally. At first, it was a concern expressed only toward members of the Christian group. Later, it was expanded to embrace others and became a wonderful part of Christian tradition.

Action to effect needed change in the status quo, however, did not develop so readily. The earliest Christian group was too small and weak to have much influence or to defend itself against opposition encountered. Jesus, while implying it in several different ways, did not make it a major priority in his teaching. Paul, who was inspired to speak of the breadth of Jesus' social concern when addressing the intellectual group on Mars Hill, apparently became discouraged when his speech did not get the results he wanted. His fateful decision to place the gospel emphasis on the more emotional level of "Jesus Christ and him crucified" (1 Cor. 2:2, NIV) had much to do with setting the course of tradition.

Not to be discounted, also, is that cultural awareness in Jesus' time did not perceive so clearly the relationship between spiritual welfare and social welfare as we are able to discern today.

Tradition, as it has been shaped in U.S. Protestantism, has been greatly influenced by the prevailing emphasis on individualism and the accompanying disparagement of controls beyond the individual. It has also been influenced by powerful convictions proclaiming that religion and politics don't mix and that unions are the enemy of the individual.

Your Temptation

You can ignore social action responsibility or place it so low on your agenda that it hardly counts and get by with little trouble. You can preach the comforting and reassuring part of the gospel, keep people feeling good about themselves, accumulate accolades, and have a smooth pastoral experience. Few people will note the oversight as long as you tend what has been called "the nursery" carefully.

If, however, you choose to take seriously the need for social action, you may expect a much rougher experience. Your congregation may resist your efforts. You will probably be criticized and some of your members will likely complain that you are neglecting your ministry and dealing in matters that do not belong to religion.

The temptation to take the easy way will be great. Will you be able to say, like Jesus, "Get thee behind me, Satan"?

The Sacred/Secular Dichotomy

It has been a long-standing practice to draw a line between the sacred and the secular aspects of culture. Religion has been concerned with the sacred while the secular has been considered outside the realm of religious concern, possibly even tainted with evil.

There is an old, negative attitude toward "the world," meaning the world of human culture. Early humans had no confidence in things they had created. They relied totally and mystically on their God, or deity, and on the diety's operations through natural phenomena. It was assumed that God was negative toward, and had no part in, the culture-building process.

The secular, therefore, was under God's judgment, but outside the realm of his primary concern. This is an unresolved theological problem that lingers in the background as social action is contemplated. There is no provision for God's interactive participation in the culture-building process. There is no clear distinction between the good and bad aspects of the so-called secular, and a question mark remains on the idea of God's love of the world.

This is a matter you will have to think and pray your way through. What is your attitude toward human culture? Is it as negative as the story of Nineveh seems to indicate? Can you see any reason why God might be working within it?

The Fixation on Life After Death

Life always has been hard, and death has been a fearful mystery. The experience of early Christians was much more acute than ours is today. Their life span was shorter, medical technology was quite limited, and harder work was necessary to get food and meet other basic needs. Going back further in time, conditions were even more severe.

It is understandable, therefore, that Christians have had a long-standing special interest in Jesus' assurances concerning life after death. The glory of the promised heavenly existence has stood in such sharp contrast to the pain and heartache of earthly experience that it has assumed a position of primacy in many people's thinking. A negative, escapist attitude has caused much neglect of social responsibility.

You will find many church members slow to respond, possibly even some opposed to, Christian social action. They will feel that the church should be concerned with spiritual matters and preparing people's souls for the experience of heaven after death.

Much patience, care, and prayerful effort may be required to help them understand the dimension of your ministry that addresses God's redemptive concern for human society as well as for the individuals who are nurtured in it.

The Conservatism of the Church

Some of the conservatism you will encounter in the church is natural and commendable. It is part of the essential function of religion as it has been developed and defined in society. The church believes that God has concern for the values by which humans live, so it sanctions and seeks to conserve those values. This is a vital function in the social process. It should be accepted and appreciated.

There is another kind of conservatism, however, that is derived from the social process. It is strong in U.S. society, where opportunity and prosperity have been so great. Many people are satisfied with the status quo and want nothing done to disturb it, nothing to rock the boat. Any attempt to effect change toward more equitable, just, or compassionate arrangements will appear to these people as a threat.

A kind of conservatism difficult to deal with is sometimes entrenched in the life of the church in a somewhat different manner. Often, people of status with vested interests in conditions the church should want to see changed hold prominent positions in the church. Frequently, they are the largest contributors and are on official boards and policy-making committees.

These people are not necessarily evil. It may be assumed that they are sincerely committed to Christ as they understand him. Do everything you can to gain their confidence and help them to mature in their understanding of the gospel and its social implications.

The Church's Institutionalism

The greatest difficulty you face may be the church's own institutionalism. Any course of action that threatens income, membership numbers, or competitive advantage can be expected to arouse fierce opposition.

This has been demonstrated many times. When the U.S. struggle for civil rights was at its height, many pastors lost their jobs when they tried to participate in a manner they understood the gospel to teach. The careers of others were tarnished or destroyed.

Pastors of major congregations at the heart of the crisis in places like Little Rock, Arkansas; Selma, Alabama; and Danville, Virginia, stayed discreetly quiet. They knew what the cost would be to their churches and to themselves if they tried to participate in the struggle.

The rationale often given for such conduct in these situations is that it is important to keep the church strong and viable for functioning after the crisis has passed. This is a good point, but it relates to the institutionalism of the church, not to the question of the church's primary mission.

The pastor of a leading Methodist church in Selma, where people who had come to march with Martin Luther King Jr., were refused admission to worship, made the point very explicit. At a later date, he spoke on a seminary campus about the Methodist ministers who, among the marchers, had made it hard for him to minister to his people.

The church is to be more than an institution. It is a body for housing the spirit of Christ. When Christ's spirit is not in it, the body is an empty shell. To continue exalting and glorifying it is to practice idolatry.

Identifying the Soul

The final difficulty is essentially a theological one. How shall the human soul be identified, and what relationship, if any, does it have to the social experience of the individual?

This is an especially serious problem when we consider that our churches have focused the concern of evangelism on the salvation of the soul. What is the soul? How is it acquired? What can affect it?

The concept is a long-standing mystery. Is it the individual's consciousness? Is it a mysterious entity, such as some early Christian thinkers had in mind when they insisted that at least a piece of bone had to be preserved always as a repository for it?

The suggestion has been made that perhaps the concept of the soul developed out of the experience of dreaming. The person who walked about in dreams seemed to be another person, and could have come to be thought of as the soul.

In your social ministry you will probably be asked, What does this particular action or event have to do with the salvation of souls? You will see no connection if you think of the soul as a separate, unaffected, indestructible entity. If you understand social experience to be capable of nurturing the spirit, influencing the development of personality and character, and having something to do with the function of consciousness, however, you will see many complicated connections of the gravest importance.

You will be forced to wonder where and what the soul is when a person is being ground down to complete demoralization by circumstances over which he or she has little or no control. What if the spark of hope and the power of control are lost? How does the soul stand apart when consciousness and character are being conditioned in twisted and distorted ways?

It probably will be difficult for you to think of the soul as being separate from all a person has become through life experiences. If this is the case, you will have no difficulty in seeing action to alter social conditions as a vital part of God's concern for salvation.

Chapter 5

Mandates for Action

There are at least three mandates for Christian social action: Scripture, the social sciences, and common sense.

Scripture and Controversy

Chapter 2 presented a brief overview of the concern found in the Bible for justice and the poor. This chapter is not a treatise on the theology of the social gospel; that has been presented by Walter Rauschenbusch and others and should no longer be necessary as justification for Christian social action.

For much of church history, Christians tended to be mystical and escapist. Then in addition they fell away from the gospel and into such follies as the Crusades and quests for political power used to exploit others. Jesus and his teachings had been greatly obscured by many addenda and reinterpretations.

Cultural currents that had been building for a long while converged dramatically in the eighteenth and the first half of the nineteenth centuries. As a consequence, the sciences came of age and humans experienced a burst of insight. The Enlightenment, sparked by physical science, was soon accompanied by the social sciences and new philosophical ventures. A massive, cultural revolution occurred.

People began to feel more competent, free, and comfortable in the world than they had ever felt before. New enthusiasm for exploration and innovation developed. All traditions were subjected to scrutiny and questioning. Religious faith was no exception.

Great interest developed in discovering the historical Jesus: what he was really like and what he actually said. The effort proved disappointing, though, because it simply was not possible. Time had obscured him in too much fog and fiction.

What did come through convincingly was that he had been a real flesh-and-blood human being. Clearly, too, he had a passion for humanity, a remarkable ethical awareness, and an obsession with the idea of the kingdom of God. His emphasis on love of neighbor, the plight of the poor, compassion, forgiveness, and peace, indicate that he had a lively interest in affairs of this life and this world, as well as in the life and world hereafter.

Theologian John Howard Yoder has said that Jesus "was a model of political action."[11] He was such a threat to the power structure of his society that he was killed for being a troublemaker.

Another point of controversy was the philosopher Hegel's introduction of his theory, the Hegelian Dialectic. It proved to be an argument for the idea of inevitable progress, which exactly fitted the spirit of the new age, especially in an eagerly booming America.

More controversy occurred when Rauschenbusch became so disturbed by the evils developing in the new industrial and rapidly growing society that he spoke out for a fresh interpretation of the gospel. Church people were questioning many church traditions, particularly the over-emphasis on otherworldliness. They grew enthused about the prevailing spirit of creativity and progress. Their enthusiasm knew no bounds.

Human society was being transformed. The kingdom of God was being brought into reality. Humans were God's children and coming into their own, as maturing recipients of God's grace. Indeed, reliance on human ability seemed to be receiving more attention than reliance on God's grace. "The world for Christ in this generation," became a popular rallying cry in inspired church circles.

Too little care was given to undergirding all of this enthusiasm with attention to theology. A clear view of the place and validity of Scripture was not maintained. The reality of sin became obscure and much of the meaning of what Christ did for the salvation of sinful humanity was neglected.

What the "Social Gospellers," as they came to be called, were doing in their careless exuberance shocked and repelled more conservative Christians. In what appeared to be less than a fully rational defensive reaction, they assumed a belligerent and emotional stance of absolute biblicism. Since their stance was orthodox and traditional, they made it their weapon of choice to slash mercilessly at their opponents.

The conservatives emphasized sin and salvation. Converts were sought through direct, persuasive, soul-saving evangelism, with the primary focus on moral behavior and life after death. Social gospel adherents sought to win people through showing Christlike concern for quality in this life. They were accused of substituting social work for evangelism.

An old definition says that heresy is overemphasis on some aspect of truth. Using this definition, both sides could be declared heretical insofar as the whole truth of the gospel is concerned.

In time, the deficiencies in both of these positions have become increasingly apparent. The theological controversy continues and seriously affects church policy, but both sides appear to have settled on more realistic attitudes toward the necessity of some measure of social action in the discharge of missional responsibility. Even so, there is much difference between them regarding types and methods of action.

Social activists are now less inclined than they once were to promote reckless humanism and give more careful attention to the Bible and theology. Conservatives, who had practiced social action on the mission field when seeking change in such matters as dress and sexual practice and had always worked at charitably meeting need, have embraced policies that promote action in politics and on some moral issues.

Although, as you will recognize, the present discussion falls heavily on the side of the social gospel, it is not intended as a partisan polemic. Instead, it seeks to look as objectively as possible at biblical themes that appear to support, even demand, action in the discharge of Christian social responsibility.

The Biblical Story

The Old Testament is the story of God's extensive involvement in the affairs of a society of people. It recounts how God was concerned with their pain and suffering. The interest he showed in their liberation from oppression became one of the central themes of the Bible.

In Jesus, God expressed his limitless concern for the whole human race, and an uninhibited willingness to inject himself into human affairs.

Jesus accepted the social focus of his religious background, but added to it a profoundly personal dimension. He agreed with his people that the love of your neighbor ranks alongside the love of God at the core of religion.

Jesus' passionate concern for human welfare was highly conspicuous, especially his concern for the poor and mistreated. His emphasis on the kingdom of God had earthly significance as well as a more spiritual meaning.

The love that Jesus so strongly advocated had a strongly social, as well as personal, dimension. Viewed in human terms, Jesus' cross was the result of his relentless interference with the social order of his day. There was a special social action implication, therefore, in his challenging declaration that those wishing to follow him must take up their crosses daily and follow his example.

After Jesus' death, resurrection, and ascension, his followers, including Peter, Paul, and many others, became notorious disturbers of their societies' status quo. The time and culture were different from our day, and they did not have our understanding of how social systems work, but there can be little doubt that they were genuine social activists.

Scripture and the Oppressed

Oppressed groups today are articulating views of the Bible and Christian faith that differ widely from what has long been accepted in the traditions of theology and the mainline churches. The strongest expressions have arisen in Latin America, where people have struggled long under dictators who have been supported by a privileged aristocracy.

Gustavo Gutierrez brought the liberation theology movement sharply to attention with the publication of his book, *A Theology of Liberation: History, Politics and Salvation.*[12] Numerous other works have expressed the view in terms of African-American theology, feminist theology, and theology related to other oppressed minorities.

Have you given thought to the perspective from which you view the Bible and its message? Or to the position from which you maintain the perspective?

Chances are that your view is from the perspective of a middle-to upper-class person who is relatively comfortable with the status quo. You may be mildly critical of things you do not like in society, but you have no passionate desire to see things changed. Can you imagine what it would be like to be subject to unrelenting prejudice and injustice?

Under such oppression, it might not be hard to view the Scriptures as a message of God's concern for his people's social liberation. At the least, this would seem no less important than God's concern for the salvation of individual souls.

The Social Science Mandate

Like Scripture, the social sciences offer a compelling mandate. Research in sociology, psychology, economics, political science, and related fields has made it clear that there are intimate relationships between social experience and personal and spiritual development.

Since Pavlov's famous experiment with dogs that illustrates how conditioning occurs, we have learned much about the effects of experience on human behavior. For example, some intimate aspects of one's being, such as personality and character, are without a doubt largely shaped and developed in response to social experience. What could be more directly related to the soul's welfare?

A ministry not taking these influences and insights into account would be both tragic and absurd. As one observer has said, "If we say that we love our fellow man as God has loved us but have no concern for an involvement in problems of human society, we are only fooling ourselves. . . . Not only must we be concerned about the persons whom we confront with the Christian gospel, but we must also be involved in changing the society which grinds men down into the dirt of crime and depravity. This is where evangelism and social concern join hands."[13]

Clearly, the scientific mandate correlates with, and lends powerful support to, the scriptural mandate. Both say you cannot have a fully responsible ministry without a wholistic view that takes the person and his or her social setting into account. Redemptive concern must focus on both.

The Mandate of Common Sense

Quite apart from requirements of Scripture and social science, common sense dictates that a serious effort to minister to people in need involves trying to remedy the conditions that are part of the reason for their need.

It strains logic to address a person's spiritual need without addressing the factors that are related to production of the need. Countless conditions affecting people's lives can either nurture them to fulfillment or cripple and destroy them.

Something is wrong when only spiritual welfare is selected for attention out of a total complex of interrelated needs.

Conclusion

You should not have difficulty finding authority to justify social action as part of your ministry. Indeed, it would take considerable mental agility to find excuses not to take such action.

Chapter 6

Preparing for Action

Meaningful social ministry requires thorough preparation. It is by no means a simple matter to be casual or superficial about. As the editor of *Circuit Rider* has said, "Preachers who believe that Christ comes to confront and transform people and communities have a battle to wage against the present day warping of human sensibilities and responses."[14]

Deliberate and thorough preparation is the ideal. Because circumstances can vary greatly, however, ideal preparation may not always be possible. Inability to follow all the steps in ideal preparation need not be an excuse for not acting in some crisis situations, however. Neither should it be an excuse for not making all preparation possible.

The following sections discuss some topics that are essential to ideal preparation. You may want to add others to the list.

Bible Study and Prayer

You need to know the Bible well enough to be sure you understand it in the broad, overall sense in which its message is best understood. Any action you take should be guided by this understanding.

There is no substitute for earnest prayer. You will need to pray at the beginning of any action you take and all along the way. You will need to pray for sensitivity and awareness to see the need for action, for a correct understanding of the issue and what is at stake, and for support as you act.

Preaching, Educating, Sensitizing

As you guide your church in its social ministry, you will need all the assistance you can get. Therefore, you should use every opportunity to inform, sensitize, and inspire members of your congregation on important issues.

Preaching provides a wonderful opportunity to stimulate and challenge people's thinking and to encourage changes in their attitudes. It is also your best chance to inspire a desire and willingness in others to become active, cross-bearing followers of Christ.

Your sermons can call attention to unjust, unloving, or generally harmful conditions in society that need to be changed. Your congregation will come to know your attitudes, expressed or implied. Your views are revealed in the sermon topics you choose, the illustrations you use and the manner in which you interpret them, and the nuances of meaning you imply in the total discourse.

Sermons can educate also, and should be harmonized with the educational objectives you have for the total church program. Of course, you should have objectives for the educational program. Make a point to encourage curriculum development and selection of literature and other resources that support active ministry concepts.

Give attention to your homiletical style. Will you stick uncritically to the Bible text, as though God has slept and nothing has changed since it was written? Will you be dully conventional, massaging individual psyches with reminders of God's grace and promises of eternal salvation? Will you emphasize histrionics and entertainment, coated with a veneer of biblical piety? Or will you do your best to be interesting, relevant to realities in society and to what people are experiencing, and firmly grounded in your best theological understandings of the spirit and message of the Bible?

If you are convinced of the biblical mandate for social action as a part of your ministry, your preaching will necessarily have a prophetic tone. Dr. J. Philip Wogaman, pastor of Foundry United Methodist Church in Washington, D.C., the congregation of President and Mrs. Clinton (and the author of the Foreword to this book), suggests a helpful set of ground rules for prophetic preaching. These include—

- highlighting the generating power of the gospel, not moralism;
- building on the political and social themes of the Bible;
- affirming the value of people;
- avoiding direct assault on the personality and reputation of individuals;
- doing homework and accurately presenting the facts and historical background of a problem;
- avoiding unsupported references or sideswiping of controversial issues;
- using church pronouncements judiciously;
- hitting an issue straight and presenting a carefully stated position;
- summarizing the opposing point of view fairly, when appropriate;
- using human illustrations but avoiding stereotypes (social preaching is very personal);
- conveying expectation that people will change, pointing to available ways to act constructively;
- recognizing that Jesus, the prophets, and the disciples aroused reaction;

- proceeding on a consensus of church officers that affirms a free pulpit against a beholden one; and
- structuring opportunity for member feedback.[15]

Be careful not to become merely a propagandist. Remember that in your efforts to educate and sensitize, you are trying to help people understand the full meaning of being Christians. You are encouraging them to grow in God's grace and to become better equipped for their ministry.

Becoming Oriented

Learn as much as you can about the setting you are operating in. What type of church are you serving? What is your community like in terms of income level, status, demographic composition, and political sentiment? What are its dominant economic features and its power structure? How adequate are its health and social services and its treatment of people with special problems and needs?

The more you know about your local community, the better prepared you will be to conduct your ministry for it. Remember, however, that your setting is in a much wider context. Your community is also your state, your nation, and the world.

Try to stay as fully informed as possible concerning significant developments in this wider arena and plan your action in terms of maximum relevance to them. As the saying goes, "Think globally and act locally."

Investigating

As noted earlier, the first practical step in social action is to get the facts. Be sure of the position you are advocating.

In many instances, of course, it will not be possible for you to do first-hand, data-gathering research. You will have to depend on secondary sources, but be careful in choosing those sources. Be sure they are the most reliable resources available. It may not be wise, for example, to put your trust in televised reports or to believe everything you read.

Analyzing

After you have gathered the facts as best you can, you are responsible to try to ascertain what the facts mean. This means you will need to remember what your anchor points are as a Christian minister.

How does the particular set of facts relate to your biblical criteria? To church tradition? To society's moral code? To community welfare? To the rights and welfare of people? To the mission and program of the church? Or to any other criteria you consider important?

It is always possible that when you weigh the factual data carefully, you may conclude they do not justify action. Prayerful consideration may convince you that the issue is not significant or that action would produce more harm than good.

Recruiting and Organizing Assistance

In addressing most issues, you will need assistance. Not only is there strength in numbers, but usually there is more work than one person can handle.

Try to recruit people you can count on. Be sure they have a thorough understanding of the project and its purpose. Give them the necessary training for their tasks.

When you recruit assistants from the membership of your congregation, you are accomplishing a double purpose: getting help and providing members opportunity for learning and spiritual growth through experience.

When at all feasible, you and your church committee should join with other people or agencies that are working on or are interested in the issues you are addressing.

Setting Priorities

Some issues are far more important that others and resources are always limited. Establishing priorities, therefore, can be an important part of preparation. Among the many issues presenting themselves for your attention, you must determine which are the most urgent and important. Be as realistic as you can when deciding.

Experience has convinced many pastors of the wisdom of working on one local issue and one broader general issue at a time. This permits maximum concentration of interest and effort.

Developing Perspective

The context in which any type of Christian action takes place is multifaceted and related to many important values. It involves church and community, society in general, various traditions, the welfare of people, and possibly many other considerations.

Before acting, you should consider how a chosen action may impinge on these values at various points. Getting a perspective on possible consequences is crucial.

Chapter 7

Major Types of Action

The action you take will be one of many types possible. Use prayer and care to select the type of action you chose for any specific situation.

Dieter T. Hessel has an excellent outline of broad general categories of types of action.[16] He calls them basic modes of social ministry. The modes he names are—

- reconciling liturgy, prayer, and proclamation;
- communal Bible study and other parish education;
- pastoral care to empower lay ministry;
- renewal of community ministry through social service, community organization, and community development;
- church involvement in public policy advocacy;
- institutional awareness of corporate responsibility.

Useful as they are, these categories are so general and vague that you will need to consider what forms of appropriate action are most suited to each mode. Several major types that should be considered in detail are discussed here. Some of them are commonly used; others are significant enough to need greater emphasis.

Providing Assistance

The church has long recognized the importance of providing assistance to those in need. The practice was common in the earliest days of church history.

One of the episodes that boosted public awareness of the early Christian movement occurred in the city of Alexandria. When a major epidemic broke out, most people able to flee, did so, leaving the sick and dying unattended. Christians, however, stayed and gave what help they could to the suffering.

It was in this spirit that Christians started hospitals and gave birth to the profession of social work. It is this same spirit that accounts for the many things Christians and churches still do to help people in need. Christian charity is widely recognized. It is an expression of loving concern, a trademark of the church.

Christian compassion prompts us to contribute to beggars on the street, to support programs that offer relief, to support the many types of helping agencies, and to support countless similar causes. For example, churches operate soup kitchens, provide food and clothing, operate housing projects, and recruit teams of members for relief work.

No doubt, the most common charitable practice is giving to people who come directly to the attention of the giver. This is the form of assistance that pastors and churches have specialized in.

Your church may provide a discretionary fund for your use in responding to requests for help. Those in crisis often turn first to their pastors. Dispensing this fund will likely provide you considerable satisfaction.

There are some negative implications associated with giving direct assistance, however, that you should be aware of. They need not discourage the practice, but they should be minimized or avoided as much as possible.

First of all, direct assistance can encourage dependency. Where at all possible, you should give primary consideration to helping people become self-reliant. This preserves self-respect and helps people maintain autonomy as responsible human beings.

In dispensing your personal or discretionary funds, you will need to avoid encouraging professional moochers. Pastors are their favorite targets. In cases where there is no personal knowledge of the circumstances, you should require references from reputable community agencies or responsible individuals.

Note also that direct aid carries an often unrecognized spiritual risk. Any kind of assistance, especially that which is delivered directly, involves power relations. People from a position of success and strength are helping those in a position of weakness, which can be embarrassing and humiliating. It threatens the recipient's self image, spiritual integrity, and sense of worth. The problem is especially serious if assistance is provided in a patronizing manner that emphasizes the difference in status between giver and receiver.

This element of risk is minimized only as the giver goes with the gift. Genuine empathy and sincere compassion imply identifying with the recipient, not an aloof act of handing down sympathy.

Recognize, too, that assistance may actually be an obstacle to true change. It may provide corporate or political interests with an excuse for not making the provisions that are their responsibility. It may beguile Christians into attitudes of complacency, assuming that others' needs are being met by their limited efforts. Having done this much, they can feel free to resist provision of more adequate assistance by government or other public sources.

Finally, you should stay aware of how complicated providing help has become. You will be challenged to become ever more creative in finding meaningful and more relevant ways of providing it.

Modern culture has become increasingly interdependent. Need in remote corners of the earth now demands as much attention as that which presents itself at your doorstep. For instance, how corporations treat employees, or what government policies precipitate may have much more to do with why some people are dependent or needy than any of the choices they themselves have the power to make.

Helping Voters

There is an Anabaptist strand of thought which leads to not voting on grounds that Christians belong first to God's kingdom, not the human "kingdoms" nations represent. This view deserves respect. At the same time, my own thinking is that voting is a major Christian responsibility. It is treated too carelessly by far too many church members. Voting is crucial to the functioning of a democracy. To neglect to vote or to remain ignorant of candidates and issues is to contribute to social breakdown and instability.

One of your responsibilities, therefore, is to make sure that your church members are impressed with the importance of casting their ballots and are given all possible help to vote wisely.

This does not mean you should promote political biases in the name of religion. That must be avoided.

The following list highlights activities that U.S. churches can engage in without fear of losing their tax-exempt status. (Some items, while legal, may call for caution and careful discernment.)

1. Churches can organize candidate forums, as long as all of the candidates are invited.

2. Church groups can meet with individual politicians to discuss issues of concern to their community.

3. Churches can and should conduct voter registration drives to encourage civic participation by caring Christians.

4. Churches can invite candidates to speak in worship services, as long as all of the candidates are invited and no fund-raising occurs.

5. Pastors may endorse candidates as long as they make it clear that the endorsement is personal and not spoken on behalf of the church.

6. Churches may distribute unbiased candidate questionnaires covering a wide range of issues, as long as the responses go to all the candidates and the answers are presented without editing or comment.[17]

Publicizing and Educating

You and your church are in a unique position to review and publicize matters of Christian and community concern. Be sure that a Christian point of view is established clearly in the minds of your church members as well as the public at large, alongside secular views. You can accomplish this thorough newspapers, leaflets, radio, television, and the Internet.

Remember, too, the public forum. It provides the opportunity to consider issues from all sides. This resource is often unavailable in communities where major issues are demanding attention. Where no other such program is available, the church can step in and make the forum a valuable means of contributing to community welfare. A regular monthly format, to which informed people would be invited to speak, could be extremely effective.

You can modify and vary the forum by having an occasional debate. To avoid generating undue controversy, you can require participants to argue for or against views that are not necessarily their own.

You can organize special study-discussion groups to consider social problems and issues; these groups would be highly appropriate for adult Sunday school classes or for re-treats. They can be planned to function on either a short-term or long-term basis.

Letter-Writing and Petitioning

Politicians, public office holders, and many agencies and businesses pay great attention to the volume and tone of mail they receive. Some even have formulas to calculate the number of opinions each letter represents.

Letter writing and petition signing, therefore, can be important means of influencing policy. Original letters composed by individual writers, are most effective. A consistent program involving an organization of lay people can become a major ministry.

In some instances, petitions can be appropriate and effective. They provide church members an opportunity to register their sentiments. Circulating petitions in the community can be a practical and helpful form of serving ministry.

Helping with Community Organization

Many North American communities are poorly organized. A skeletal political structure usually fails to view the community in wholistic terms or to assume responsibility for more than a limited number of community needs. Agencies and services are often so fragmented and uncoordinated that they appear to be a confusing jumble rather than a functional network focused on improving citizens' quality of life.

As a result, many needs go unmet. People with needs find themselves on a treadmill, shunted from one agency to another.

The church can help do something about this. It can be a nerve center of the community, sensing when people are hurting and acting to improve service provisions.

You yourself should be able to find ways of functioning as an unofficial community organizer. As a pastor, you qualify to some degree automatically as a community leader. You can make the role what you will. If you decide to confine your ministry to the internal affairs of your church, the role can be almost meaningless. You will be considered much like a tribal chief who builds high walls around himself and his people. The arrangement protects, but it also isolates.

If, however, you take a sensibly disciplined, participatory interest in the community, you will be viewed quite differently. You will be considered a dynamic leader of a church-related group of citizens who have a concern for the community. This, you will discover, gives your ministry greatly expanded significance. You will be received in a manner that will give you and your church many opportunities for effective influence in the direction of your Christian concerns.

A reputation for sincere concern will qualify you to function as an unofficial community organizer. You can fulfill this role without neglecting responsibilities to your church. In fact, it can become an important part of your pastoral role, an invigorating aspect of your duty to, for, and with your church. It will give you opportunities to exert a constructive influence from within the community structure— quite a contrast to standing outside as an unhappy critic.

A rule observed by professional community organizers, however, should be taken seriously. Professionals discipline themselves to work quietly, often behind the scenes, to reach goals or effect needed change. They do not demand or expect credit for accomplishment. They often try to bring other people into the effort, so those others can receive the credit and increase in stature as community leaders.

Do not become a prima donna, seeking power and the spotlight; those who demand attention and credit are seldom fully effective.

Another important dimension of organizing involves preparing the local church to effectively fulfill its social ministry responsibility. Depending on the situation, the difficulty of this task will vary. Some situations will require more skills and effort to organize and implement than others.

Your responsibility will be to build interest and support, to recruit competent and interested lay members, and to help design structure and choose projects.

Where at all possible, lay people should be in charge of organizing the projects. You should stand by, give support, work with the groups, and see that the congregation stays informed of their groups' activities.

Empowering

Some kinds of injustice imposed on people can best be remedied by the people themselves. They have the power to make changes, but are unable to exert it. Their need is derived from a lack of vision, hope, and organization.

They can, however, learn, with guidance, to hope, organize themselves, and fight for their rights. The late Saul Alinsky, a Jewish social worker, demonstrated the effectiveness of this type of action. It merits serious consideration by Christians concerned about social justice.

Empowerment provides the opportunity for close identification with those being helped and minimizes paternalism.

Advocating

People suffer many different kinds of injustice. Sometimes they are in no position to do anything about their situation. You and your church can help them by analyzing their plight and becoming their advocates.

Doing this, you provide more than temporary relief with tokens of assistance. You are identifying more closely with those you are helping.

Too often, the poor and other victims of injustice suffer in silence. No one pays attention to their plight. They have no one to represent them. What could be more directly relevant to what Jesus said about being concerned for the hungry, the sick, and the outcasts of society locked up in prisons? An unbelievable number of such sufferers are found throughout society, and they are generously represented in nearly every community. Often, only Christians with heart-sensitized eyes bother to see them.

Advocacy may be appropriate where the need of only a single individual is involved, or it can be used in behalf of groups of any size, and it can provide support for various types of causes.

Protesting

When the nature of a situation is such that other forms of action seem inappropriate, one of the many forms of protest can be used. This mode of action is direct, confrontational, and always available. It publicizes conditions and can often be effective in producing needed change.

Protesting is such a natural way of reacting that it can take many forms that vary in effectiveness. Common forms of protest are picketing, striking, marching, rallying, impeding, resisting, and boycotting.

Cooperating

Remember that other people and agencies within your community are also working for its welfare. You and your church should cooperate with them. This can be a significant form of social action. It speaks loudly of genuine concern for human welfare.

Community organizers have often complained that ministers and churches are uncooperative. This is not only a bad image to have, it is also bad churchmanship and a poor expression of Christianity. Work with community organizers so you and your church won't bear this reputation.

Conclusion

You probably will never have occasion to use all of these types of action. It will be well to keep them in mind, however, and be prepared to employ them appropriately as needed. Selecting the best mode of action can be critical in determining the desired outcome of any situation. Ordinarily the selection will not be made by you individually, but in consultation with the group of people with whom you are working.

Chapter 8

Guiding the Church in Its Social Ministry

The tunnel vision of the church—its narrow parochialism—is a problem that has been long recognized. Reuel Howe commented on it succinctly in 1964.

"Both clergy and laity," he said, "think of the church in terms of the local congregation and its internal concerns . . . The relation to the world of politics, law, and custom is either not thought of at all or done ambiguously. Neither is there awareness among many people of the meaning being expressed by the plastic and performing arts, by science and industry, and the significance they have for the meanings of the Gospel. The parochialism of this image of the church often reduces Christian faith and practice to the dimensions of a cult."[18]

The Alban Institute Church and Community Project, described earlier, identified three elements as crucial for congregations wishing to be effectively involved in their communities. These elements were tradition, organization, and inspiration. Every successful project involved "advocates for tradition, an administrative committee, and a visionary leader who is the essential source of inspiration."[19]

Special emphasis belongs on the third of these elements. Other than your responsibility to your Lord, your primary responsibility is to the church where you are the pastor. You are its leader, guide, inspirer, instructor, educator, equipper, and servant. The congregation needs your prayerful, thoughtful, and informed best in all aspects of its program, including provisions for meeting its social responsibility.

The church is, by definition, the body of Christ in the world. Like Jesus, it has a responsibility to and for the world. Its purpose is to proclaim that God loves the world, seeks to bring his kingdom to reality in it, and is concerned to save all of its inhabitants. At the same time, the church is an institution. As with other institutions and social structures, it can be infiltrated by sin and evil.

Critics of the church often say that churches talk about being concerned for the poor and mistreated, but do little to change the systems in society that cause human misery. Instead, churches tend to identify themselves with the relatively prosperous middle class, it is charged, and to enjoy their comfortable place in the status quo.

Because social action is an integral part of the church's ministry, your success as a pastor will depend largely on how well you enable your congregation to meet this part of its responsibility. Far from being an unwelcome burden, this can be one of the most interesting and challenging aspects of your ministry. It ties in perfectly with your concern to save souls and proclaim the good news of the gospel.

The ideal church will be theologically literate, spiritually aware, evangelically and socially active. Since the ideal is usually more goal than reality, you must pursue it to the best of your ability. All aspects of the church's functioning are important, but social action is the part most often neglected.

You will be fortunate if you are privileged to serve a church that has a well-organized and active social ministry.

In all probability, however, this will not be the case. You will need to prepare, therefore, to try to develop such a ministry.

A starting point might be to organize a small study-discussion group to explore ideas included in social ministry. The writings of some of the church's critics who are engaged in struggles for justice could stimulate lay interest and provide a good basis for discussion. To weigh provocative statements such as the following, for example, could prove quite profitable:

Frank Chikane charges that the church, historically, has tended to take sides with the dominant classes of society, that is, the people who, for the most part, have been responsible for the exploitation, misery, and even death of many of the weak and powerless.[20]

James H. Cone, the articulate proponent of black liberation theology, deplores the preaching of sermons about justice and praying for liberation and fair treatment for all, while doing nothing tangible to make the verbal affirmations reality. It is, he says, just "a farce." The church, Cone says, gives sanction to prevailing aspects of culture, offering little criticism, either theological or moral.[21]

In his letter from the Birmingham jail, Martin Luther King Jr. expressed disappointment that the religious leaders of the city would not stand with him in the struggle for justice. He thought they should be able to see the rightness of the cause and help get the system changed. He was distressed that many church people, instead of recognizing the significance of the national struggle for racial and economic justice, were standing back and saying, "Those are social issues with which the gospel has no real concern."

King protested that such an attitude sprang from an otherworldly religion which has become all too prevalent in the churches. It was, he added, part of a strange distinction between body and soul, things sacred and things secular.

The tragedy, King felt, was that so near the beginning of a new millennium, the church, the total religious community, stands "largely adjusted to the status quo . . . a taillight behind other community agencies rather than a headlight leading man to higher levels of justice."[22]

There are, of course, many other ways of getting your church started in social ministry, some of which were diussed previously. If social ministry becomes a matter of primary concern, creative ideas will occur to you. Make it a matter of conscious intent in all that you do: in preaching, liturgy, education, and all other forms of communication. Encourage the use of banners, symbols, and the like to create an atmosphere of concern in the sanctuary. Have lay people make relevant reports and announcements.

In his excellent book on *Social Ministry*, Dieter T. Hessel, has a lengthy list of principles for use in social education. He lists them under the headings of worship, study and nurture, and action.

With respect to worship, he suggests incorporating social concerns into the total worship experience, and incorporating worship into all aspects of study and action. In addition, he mentions making creative use of holidays and special events to emphasize social concerns, and encourages making social concerns the focus of personal and family devotions.

Under study and nurture, he stresses the importance of including social education in the Sunday church school, with appropriate attention to biblical and theological considerations.

Hessel also mentions activating small covenant or contract groups for specific social mission objectives and providing special study opportunities for the management of social relations and for training leadership for social action.

In the action category, he lists involving the whole church as fully as possible by stressing social focus in all aspects of the educational curriculum, by celebrating the focus in worship, and by having all covenant and growth groups add social action to their study and worship. He also suggests supporting individual members in their on-the-job ministries, focusing congregational worship, and encouraging study and action on major social concerns, particularly those receiving denominational and ecumenical attention.[23]

Helping lay members in their ministry should receive particular attention. After all, they are the ones who will be responsible for implementing the church's social ministry program. If they are already prepared for action, your task is one of assisting them, in which case, the title of this chapter should begin with the word "assist" rather than "guide."

It is likely, however, that you will have to recruit and train lay people for the ministry of action. Even those members already committed to action will need the benefit of further training. Everyone will need to sharpen their skills for teamwork and be organized into functional units with well-defined responsibilities.

You can start with a small corps of people whose obvious interests and abilities qualify them to work within a unit. Enlist, train, organize, and involve them in action. Let their effort be the means of further recruitment.

Training can be accomplished in many ways: through formal study-discussion sessions over an extended period, through activities that are concentrated in retreats, or possibly through exercises or projects that incorporate learning-by-doing. Maximum use should be made of resources the denominational leadership can provide. Consider, also, local professionals who can lend expertise such as social workers, schoolteachers, family counselors, psychiatrists, judges, law enforcement officers, and others.

Training and organization for total ministry have been impressively combined in the program of the Church of the

Savior in Washington, D.C. You probably will be unable to duplicate this model with the usual, already-established congregation, but it provides a challenging ideal. The principles it incorporates are worthy of imitation.

The congregation at the Church of the Savior was started by a thoughtful young Baptist minister who was just home from World War II, and had deep misgivings about how most traditional churches were functioning. The program of this church combines deep spirituality, effective evangelical outreach, and strikingly innovative social ministry.

Intensive study and preparation in its School of Christian Living are required before a member is admitted. Serious commitment to clearly defined obligations is also a part of the admission process. This assures that all members are committed to actively support the total program, of which social action is a significant part.

The church limits the number of its members, creating spin-off groups as its membership becomes too great for efficient functioning. Its style of organization is one of its most innovative features.

Permanent organizational structures are kept to a minimum. Instead, Church of the Savior relies on ad hoc "missions" continuously being formed and re-formed from among its membership. These missions function until their purpose has been fulfilled; then they are dissolved.

Dialogic, non-traditional worship, along with intensive attention to nurturing in spiritual formation and growth, have equipped the members for exceptional effectiveness in their varied ministries.

Another example of unusual structure and organization is that of the Community of Christ the Servant in Lombard, Illinois. This congregation was established as an experiment by the Board of American Missions of the Lutheran Church in America.

The congregation meets in a barn and has no intention of constructing a permanent, traditional church building. The church gives nearly fifty percent of its budget to benevolences, and asks its members to join and influence secular organizations rather than to form committees and organizations within the congregation.

It strives for uniqueness in its philanthropic projects. One of its most unusual efforts is the help it provides a Chicago youth gang called the Black Disciples. The church provides the gang advice and funds for various business enterprises. For other projects, the barn and its equipment are made available to a wide variety of community groups.[24]

Organization in more traditional churches can take any number of forms. You will need to consider many variables, such as the size and resources of your church, the type of community where it is located, current issues of local and global concern, special interests of your congregation, and denominational emphases and beliefs.

The specific structure is not as important as having clearly defined objectives and keeping people informed about what their duties are. Leadership should be in the hands of lay members whenever possible.

A few examples follow that show innovative organizational arrangement in more or less traditional churches that suggest the range of possibilities.

When Martin Luther King Jr., became pastor of the Dexter Avenue Baptist Church in Montgomery, Alabama, the congregation followed his creative leadership in structuring a more tightly organized, sharply focused, and responsible organization. In the process, attention was focused both inwardly and outwardly. Internally, a centralized budget was established, along with a well-organized program to assure financial support. All of the members were organized into twelve clubs, according to the months in which their birthdays fell. Each club had a number of important duties to perform, and competition between them in support of church programs heightened the level of interest in many activities.

Outreach programs left no question of the church's interest in and involvement with circumstances in the surrounding community. A social and political action committee was charged with responsibility to promote membership in the NAACP and to sponsor forums and mass meetings for the discussion of issues before elections. The goal was established to have every member of the congregation become a registered voter. A committee was appointed to raise money for an annual college scholarship for a deserving high school graduate of the congregation. A nursery for small children was established, and a committee was organized to work on recruitment of new members.[25]

Another innovative plan with community relevance was developed by the Social Action Committee of Atlanta's First Congregational Church. Members of the committee were divided into three groups: "sitters," "joiners," and "helpers."

The "sitters" attended meetings of such various civic groups as the school board and city council. Their presence in the meetings was to remind the groups that the larger community, especially the church, was concerned with their policies and actions. After sitting, observing, and listening, they reported to the committee and, through the committee, to the congregation.

The "joiners" joined various local civic organizations and groups seeking to bring about reforms. They performed an interlocking and coordinating function, helping the church to relate to groups it shared a common interest with.

The "helpers" sought worthwhile projects underway in the community and enlisted their own services. The projects included programs to provide low cost housing and to get people registered to vote. The helpers gave the church a special kind of public presence and favorable image.[26]

The Park Place Church of God in Anderson, Indiana, developed a most elaborate and comprehensive program. Out of concern for the church scattered as well as the church gathered, it added a Minister of Outreach to its staff. Then it set about studying the community around the church to discover the human hurts living there. This enabled members "to fulfill their identity through ministering at the point of those hurts."

After identifying a geographic area of responsibility and the human needs in that area, a serious effort was made to develop projects that fit the needs. The Board of Evangelism reviewed the findings of the study and identified sixty-six possible projects. From this list, ten projects that seemed most important were selected. A principle that was firmly agreed on was that no project would be initiated that duplicated or competed with an existing service, though supplementary assistance might be given where it seemed needed by a service already in operation.

Ten task forces were established, each to carry out a specific project. The task forces were identified as the following:

1. *Control:* to provide the total community with a telephone service that any person with any need could call to get help.

2. *Big Brothers and Sisters:* to recruit members to befriend a child or youth. The adult/child pair woule spend time together at least weekly. The children and youth would be identified and referred by the Community Guidance Center, the Department of Public Welfare, the Juvenile Parole Office, and Family Service.

3. *Fellowship of St. Luke:* to befriend people who are homebound because of age or health.

4. *Open Mind:* to relate on a one-to-one basis to children and youth who have learning disabilities.

5. *Open Lap:* to involve members in service to one of the day care centers for children on at least a half-day-per-week basis.

6. *Fellowship of the Cup of Cold Water:* to create a pool of members with a variety of skills to provide help when and where needed in such areas as transportation, carpentry, plumbing, yard work, house work, and income tax consultation.

7. *Bridge Builders:* to build bridges of understanding and cooperation between blacks and whites in the community.

8. *Fellowship of the Open Door:* to work on a one-to-one basis with parolees, providing friendship, help with employment, help with finding housing, and so on.

9. *Friendship:* to participate in Thursday evening discussion meetings or Sunday morning classes at the reformatory.

10. *Fellowship of St. Andrew:* to work with prospects for church attendance, cultivate friendship with them, discover and remove barriers to their attendance.

Membership on these ten task forces was open to all church members who were willing to commit themselves to the task and the necessary preparation.

An additional set of specialized task forces was created to be made up of members with special skills and experience work at a variety of goals. Among them was to study the feasibility of setting up a lending facility for the poor, to investigate the possible need for an outpost center to channel people with needs to appropriate service agencies, to form a corporation to provide for housing needs, and to seek improvement of living conditions for migrant farm workers.[27]

These examples are thoughtful and creative. They show how organization for social ministry can be adapted to local situations and needs.

Conspicuously missing in most of these organizational plans cited are those that address issues beyond the local community. The local community is envisioned well, but the global one is dimly seen, if at all.

This is a major weakness in the vision and ministry of most local churches. It is especially serious in light of today's global connectedness. In the modern, interdependent world, individuals and local communities are often as profoundly affected by circumstances far away as they are by events in the local community.

What happens in Washington, Geneva, Tokyo, Moscow, or some corporate board office, to say nothing of what is circulated in the mass media, can be enormously important to human welfare. Churches need to stay aware of the risks and dangers. Their organizational structure should allow their members to always be aware of the broader issues, and should provide an avenue to wrestle with the value problems involved.

Conditions affecting social justice are especially prevalent. Since they are so closely related to the core of the Christian faith, they should never be overlooked or tolerated without the church making its opposition known.

One would think it should be easy to move the church to act for social justice. This, however, is not always the case. The subject of false imprisonment, for example, or the production of land mines and nuclear weapons is so far removed from the personal experience of many church members that it is difficult to arouse their interest in it. Members who have financial interests to protect may oppose consideration of fair wages and a more equitable distribution of wealth.

Recall that with economic issues as well as other matters, you may encounter opposition. Often oppositional members have either financial or intellectual commitments to protect, which make them satisfied with the status quo.

Be patient with these members and assure them of your sincere effort to understand their position, but be firm and as open as possible in holding to your own convictions, which, it is hoped, will be governed by reasonable biblical insight and Christian ethical principles.

Actually, it may be unrealistic to expect consensus on any position where values are involved. When you are prayerfully assured of the right thing to do, there will be times when you have to move forward with whatever support you are able to secure.

Be careful to maintain a Christian spirit of kindness and respect toward opposition, but do not be intimidated by it. After prayerfully weighing the importance of an issue, do not let the desire for peace and harmony be the final consideration.

Be sure to keep in mind the church's own economic practices, which are especially important where action advocating economic justice is being considered. Are church employees being paid reasonable wages? Does the church give consideration to the needs of working class people when requiring union or non-union services? Is the church careful in its claims of tax exemption?

You will find that it is wise for the church not to spread its social ministry efforts too thin. Concentrating on one or two major issues at a time is usually best. One local and one global would seem ideal. The issues chosen for action should receive the full support of the church's energy and influence.

In this regard, the church's usual charitable assistance—that which is done by tradition and almost automatically—should not be counted. This type of help does not ordinarily require much overt action. The same can be said for the taking of special offerings for various good causes. There is not much action involved in giving a token amount of money occasionally.

Charitable help has much more meaning when it involves members getting to know and identifying with those in need. Jesus emphasized "coming unto" and "visiting." Likewise, the cause that needs money also needs in-depth study, understanding, and all possible action involvement of the giver.

There is a challenge the church needs to hear in the words of Cesar Chavez when he was leading the struggle of migrant workers for better wages and working conditions. His pointed statement was,

> We ask for the church's presence with us, beside us, Christ among us. We ask for the church to sacrifice with the people for social change, for justice, and for love of neighbor. We don't ask for words, we ask for deeds. We don't ask for paternalism, we ask for servanthood.[28]

Let me finish the chapter with these further suggestions:

1. Keep your church from the narrow vision that sees the community around it in less than wholistic terms, as primarily a hunting ground, or as a place of opportunity for the enhancement of its pride and institutionalism.

2. Do not duplicate or compete with existing services.

3. Emphasize the importance of cooperation.

4. Keep lay people in the lead at every point possible.

5. Maximize publicity of the ministry of lay people in their everyday, on-the-job activities.

6. Do not lose sight of the reality of sin, in people or in social structures. Keep the church mindful that all social action it engages in is an extension of the ministry of Jesus in conveying the word of God's love and redeeming grace.

7. Remember professor Richard Niebuhr's words concerning the purpose of the church: that it is to "increase among [people] the love of God and neighbor."[29]

A student whose commute to seminary took him through a blighted area of a major city reflected on how many churches he saw along the way. What were the churches doing, he asked? Why had they not made more of a difference in the area around them? How did they justify their existence? The church buildings seemed extravagant for the neighborhood. The student wondered whether some of the money used for the church buildings and other institutional programs couldn't have been used to improve the quality of the housing in the area. He expressed the feeling that there must be something terribly wrong in a situation where so much human need was so obviously apparent in the shadow of so many churches.[30]

A man who visited Moscow during the days of communist control made a similar observation. Standing one day in front of his hotel near the Kremlin wall, he said he had counted more church spires looming on the skyline than he had ever seen in one place before.

Most of the church buildings were vacant or being used as warehouses or museums, he was informed. He could not keep from wondering what kind of influence the churches had exerted before communism took over.

Surely, you and your church can find ways of conducting a social ministry of greater significance.

Chapter 9

Areas of Day-to-Day Concern

Some churches show little concern for social ministry, limiting themselves to words and occasional acts of charity. But even those congregations that are sincerely involved find so many things demanding attention that they have to choose among them. No church can do everything.

Priorities often are determined by special circumstances of time and place. The presence of migrant workers, a garment factory, a liquor store, or slot machines in a community, for example, can influence the choice of project.

The size of a congregation's membership and the extent of its resources are important factors. Levels of education, professional backgrounds, and social status will have an effect. Special interests of those with strong personalities in the membership may account for some choices.

Regardless of how and why the choices are made, certain forms of activity have become more or less habitual with churches. Some, in fact, have become so habitual that they are stereotyped and discredited to some extent as being the only activity expected of the church.

This does not mean that you should abandon such concerns, but that you should try to find new and better ways for the church to pursue them. Working on situations before they become major problems can preclude confrontations at a later time.

Even in the case of the most commonly pursued problem, failures in persistence and consistency can impair effectiveness. Follow-through is crucial. When short-term problems are resolved, their demise can be celebrated. When first efforts do not resolve a matter of long-term duration, however, the church should not let it drop or quietly accept defeat.

The following needs have frequently been of concern to action-conscious churches. Some of the items will likely require your attention at one or more junctures in your ministry. You will be better able to respond if you have thought about these issues ahead of time and considered how you may want to handle them (with the understanding that you will not be the only decision-maker).

Providing Assistance

Providing assistance has been mentioned before. It is a problem that arises in many different forms. Churches have responded to it in an equal variety of ways, from quickie handouts to carefully planned extensive programs providing aid on a continuous basis.

Little is being done in an organized way, however, either by local churches or by denominations, to effect change in public policy so that more adequate and sensitive provisions meet welfare needs. This would not be as satisfying as giving assistance directly, but it could produce far greater benefits.

In addition to helping those in need with food, clothing, shelter, employment, and the like, the church can help them find other sources of help that may be more appropriate than the church. Referral should be accompanied with gestures that communicate respect and sincere interest.

The multiple resources that are often referred may be so scattered that physically getting to them is difficult and confusing. Providing transportation, helping with writing letters, explaining documents, preparing tax reports, and the like can be important forms of aid.

A church is seldom prepared to give long-term assistance with economic needs. It has other resources, however, both material and spiritual, that it can provide in abundance—if it has the spirit for it.

Sharing spiritual resources requires even more care than sharing material things. For example, a hungry person may not appreciate your efforts to convert him or her to your religion. Even if the person submits, it may be with insincerity, even cynicism. The Chinese had a term for their compatriots who became enticed by missionary handouts. They called them "Rice Christians."

In addition to assisting the destitute, it is important to remember the many needy people who are doing their best to get by without charity. They are the vast number of working poor whose wages are not sufficient to enable them to live with dignity and reasonable comfort in a society running wild with indulgence. Millions of them and their families are living below or barely above the poverty line. They and their children are ill clothed, ill fed, poorly housed, and often without needed medical care.

These worthy poor should weigh heavily on the church. In every responsible way possible, the church should exert its influence for economic justice, that is, for fairer wages and a more equitable distribution of wealth. This responsibility is especially significant because many churches are made up of relatively comfortable middle-class people, while the poor are much less significantly represented.

The best place to express this kind of Christian charity is at the voting booth and in the halls of legislatures. The church might well consider getting involved in politics to address the plight of the poor.

Alcohol

Alcohol use, like that of tobacco and illegal drugs, merits the serious attention of the church. Since the debacle of Prohibition, the church's voice against alcohol has often been muted. Church members may voice opposition to the location of a liquor store or vote to keep their town dry, but it is generally assumed that people, even church members, will drink if they want to. When this occurs, moderation is advocated; drunk driving is opposed.

Unfortunately, few churches are willing to face the high personal and social costs of alcohol consumption. They are opposed to it, of course, but their temper is not up about it.

Many Christians were embarrassed and humiliated by the unhappy outcome of Prohibition. The memory of that failure lingers on. No good replacement plan for controlling alcohol production and distribution has been devised.

Church leaders appear intimidated by the stigma of this history. They are reluctant to come out too strongly against alcohol for fear of being castigated as prohibitionists. They seem to have settled down in resignation, at the same time letting the imbibers and the liquor industry have their way.

Yet problems associated can be alcohol acute and should continue to be a major concern of the church. Since the old ways of opposing them have become stereotyped and ineffective, new and better ways should be sought.

Give greater emphasis to courses in the church school that address alcohol, and work to improve the courses' contents. Encourage lay people to make better and fuller use of the mass media for discussion of alcohol consumption. A stronger expression of sensible, rational, Christian value concern can be fostered.

Another approach identifies alcohol as the dehumanizing agent it can so easily become. This approach carries the weight of theological, psychological, and sociological argument in its favor and can be effective if given maximum emphasis.

When ingested, alcohol goes almost immediately and directly to the frontal part of the brain, the cortex. This is the part of the brain that controls consciousness, thought, valuing, and inhibitions. It is the seat of conscience and what Freud called the superego. Alcohol tends to numb the cortex and put it out of operation.

Drinking alcohol, therefore, can be a symbolic representation of desire to resign from the human race. In moderate amounts, it indicates only a limited desire—to escape temporarily the tensions of living. In larger amounts, however, it can indicate a masochistic or suicidal inclination.

Alcohol is a drug that produces tempting pleasurable sensations and may even, according to recent research, have modest beneficial in addition to damaging effects on our bodies. It is accompanied, however, by a subtle addictive influence. People often become trapped in it. Their lives, in terms of the potential God originally invested in them, can then be effectively destroyed.

This is the point that legitimizes Christian concern. It can provide the foundation for efforts you and your church make against use of alcohol and the alcohol-producing industry.

You probably will have considerable experience with those addicted to alcohol. Deal compassionately with them; give them all the help you can, but be on guard against manipulation by them. Penitence and contrition when they are drunk can be forgotten quickly when they are sober.

The public is increasingly aware of the needless deaths and other damage caused by drunk drivers and is working to make the situation better. The problem still exists, however, and should be a matter for prayerful concern of churches and church members.

Gambling

Gambling is a social problem that has been around for a long time, yet it appears to be growing especially acute in present-day American society. It was evident at the scene when Jesus was being crucified, and it is an increasing obsession in our society as the growing number of lotteries, casinos, slot machines, betting parlors, and numerous other accommodating arrangements testify.

Gambling is part of the North American obsession with money and with the chance to obtain money in a manner as far removed as possible from earning it. People who work hard for their money are often made to feel foolish. Many are enticed to seek it in some unearned fashion: the more explicitly by a straight run of gambling luck, the better.

As with many other issues, you and the church will not be able to eliminate the problem of gambling. You can, however, identify and highlight its idolatrous implications, its social costs, and its moral effects of alienation and disregard for other people.

Abortion

Abortion is an especially sensitive issue that puzzles and divides sincerely concerned Christians. There is no happy road through the issues it raises. Abortion involves opposing sets of values, each of which can be interpreted as absolute.

You are fortunate if you never have to become personally involved with this issue. It is a matter of deep concern, both to individuals and society. Only God can know the best resolution.

Is it better to have a child brought into the world with reasonable promise of sufficient love and physical care to provide for a meaningful and fulfilled life? Or should every conception be brought to term regardless of life prospects? Should all responsibility be left to God, or does he expect humans to accept some of the responsibility?

Prayer for insight into God's will is certainly called for, and an interim ethic rooted in mournful decision-making may have to be the answer.

Homosexuality

Homosexuality is probably the one issue today causing the most distress in churches at the present time. Few denominations have escaped controversy and divisiveness on the subject.

No doubt the prominence of this issue is due in part to the mass media's treatment of it. It may also be due in part to the anonymity in its urbanization and a more legal tolerance of homosexuals, which removes some of the previous onus of embarrassment.,

Homosexual behavior goes against longstanding moral standards and sensitivities. Reaction against it is, therefore, understandable. Discrimination against homosexual people, however, is another matter, which should be of concern in the context of both Christianity and democracy.

Ambiguity and emotion surround the question of the etiology, or causes, of the behavior. No convincing evidence has been found to settle the question.

In such a situation, dogmas become rooted easily. They are weapons devised in the quest for advantage in debate. Beware of them. Insofar as you and the church are concerned, your decisions should be preceded by much humble prayer for guidance with freedom from stereotypes and prejudices.

Family Life

Churches have always had special interest in the quality of family life. They have laid claim to privileges in defining and controlling marriage, divorce, christening, and many other important aspects of family life. They have been profoundly concerned with regulation of behavior between the sexes, with the nurture and training of children, and with parent-child relationships.

Many churches, however, do not have a well organized, carefully planned program to help sustain and strengthen families. This is a type of ministry that needs much more attention.

When Roy Burkhart was pastor of the First Community Church in Columbus, Ohio, he developed a creative program. It began with children at the junior high school level and continued through adult marriage counseling. Actually, a nursery and program for younger children were provided also, but serious constructive work began with junior high students. From that point, it developed by logical steps to the adult level.

The most qualified people available worked with the junior high school students to help them understand their personalities and how they interacted with others. Personality inventories were used to ascertain each child's personality profile, which was then carefully interpreted to the child. Programs were developed to help them understand sex and boy-girl relationships, along with many other matters of special interest to teens and pre-teens. Parents were informed and consulted at appropriate intervals. An attempt was made to support teaching objectives with other relevant and interesting activities.

For the next age level, even greater emphasis was placed on understanding personality and the differences in the ways personalities functioned. Dating practices were given much attention and Christian ideals for sexual relations were emphasized.

Older youth and young adults were provided with programs related to mate selection and pre-marital counseling. Preparation for marriage and family life was heavily emphasized. Married couples were offered programs on marital relations and on parent-child relationships.

You may not be able to do all of these things, but they constitute a model worthy of emulation. Emphasizing a Christian family life is sufficiently important to justify a major investment of creative effort.

At-Risk Youth

Closely related to concern for family life is the concern for of troubled young people, those sometimes described as "at risk." Some churches have given special attention to them. Some years ago, the Methodist Board of Social Concerns assigned this author to write a book on the subject and made it a study emphasis throughout the denomination.[31]

Recent tragic examples of youth violence underscore the importance of addressing the concern. Our society's neglect of its children, vividly exemplified in juvenile crime, shocks the sensibilities of even the most complacent church.

The growing spirit of alienation in our society, which fosters indifference toward one another, finds expression in hostile attitudes and intolerance toward all lawbreakers, even the youngest. Punishment is the prevailing mood. Less and less thought is being given to rehabilitation and salvation.

Most of the public seems quite prepared for serious young offenders to be tried as adults—that is, in a more punitive frame of reference. This general attitude of punitiveness is challenged far too little by Christians and churches. What about the Bible's message that God is love, that every human soul is of inestimable worth, that God's saving grace is available to every sinner at every stage of life, and that the church is commissioned to spread this message of hope and redemption to all the world?

Instead of giving up on so many lives, consigning them to the human trash heap, or the ever more popular execution chamber, Christians and church members are called to affirm their faith in the reality of God's saving grace.

Every young life is especially important, even the life of one who has committed the most heinous crime. The adult world cannot simply punish the one who offends and wash its hands of responsibility, as Pilate did.

Admittedly, juvenile crime is a serious and often baffling problem, one that challenges the church at its gospel roots. There are no simple, easily applied answers. The gospel's prescription of love, socially applied love of neighbor, is the only one holding promise that anything positive can be done about it.

The gist of what has been said here can be applied also to adult criminal offenders. It is just more obviously relevant to juveniles.

Your church can find numerous practical ways of approaching the problem. The first, obviously, will be to educate yourself. Study the literature. Gather statistical reports and newspaper articles. Inquire at police headquarters, social agencies, and the juvenile court. Interview judges, schoolteachers, administrators, and other knowledgeable people.

Find out who and how well trained the people are who function at thresholds of entry when juvenile offenders are first apprehended. How sensitive are these people? What care is taken to cause as little trauma as possible so that antisocial grudges are avoided?

These are conditions one or more people should try to stay knowledgeable about and keep the church informed on—

- the extent of juvenile delinquency and crime in the local community and the nation;
- the process youthful offenders go through at the time of apprehension;
- the conditions of incarceration and treatment;
- the extent and seriousness of rehabilitative efforts;
- the adequacy of the juvenile court;
- the exact nature of laws relating to offenses by juveniles.

Some states have Family Courts instead of Juvenile Courts; some employ a variety of arrangements to have juvenile cases channeled through a tangential function of other courts. In any case, the juvenile treatment branch is often the least well supported in the judicial system.

The effort to establish and maintain a sensitive, caring, rehabilitative system for the treatment of juveniles is constantly under attack by people with rigidly punitive and legal orientation.

The public's usual inclination is to have young offenders punished severely in the hope that it will prevent them from repeating their offenses. When the treatment fails, as it frequently does, the next impulse is to get them out of sight, which usually means put them in some type of institution, the farther away the better, where they will, presumably, be given treatment. Unfortunately, there are seldom enough holding institutions; they are nearly always overcrowded, and the quality of treatment provided in them is not a priority.

Inevitably, many youthful offenders are released on probation, which has tended to be almost a farce. Probation officers are nearly always underpaid and overloaded with cases. They usually do well to maintain occasional contacts with their cases. What they can accomplish in the way of rehabilitation is almost nil.

Currently, little public interest is invested to learn the root causes of juvenile delinquency. Little interest is shown in linking the treatment process with Christian ethical ideals. The nation's churches need to provide he impetus for this to happen. If they fail, which among the nation's other institutional structures could be expected to assume the responsibility?

Housing

Many churches are seriously involved in efforts to provide housing. Some recruit youth to spend vacation time helping rehabilitate housing in deteriorating areas. Some help provide new homes, often in cooperation with an organization such as Habitat for Humanity. A few cooperate with government agencies in providing and operating multiple housing projects.

You, as pastor, will probably need to have at least a modicum of information about the methods and merits of the various types of housing programs operating in your community and elsewhere (so you know what could be going on in your community if it's not already). Hopefully, you will have qualified lay people that will take the initiative and direct your church's participation.

Peace Initiatives

Though religion has been the cause of much conflict, the church has always been concerned about peace. This concern has been expressed in many ways. Preaching, liturgy, Christian education, and church literature have been devoted to it. It has been a major topic of forums, seminars, and study groups. Marches have been sponsored and protest groups have been organized with a focus on military installations, arms manufacturing plants, nuclear facilities, and the like.

The church has held human life to be sacred and considers killing abhorrent. Yet Christians and churches have found it difficult to abide by Jesus' teaching about forgiveness and turning the other cheek. In general, they have been more inclined to yield to self-interest and ethnocentric impulses when situations of conflict arise.

Patriotism often causes national loyalty to take precedence over Christian commitment. This, you will find, can be a difficult matter to deal with. There is no simple, easy solution. Churches in Germany either supported Hitler or gave assent by staying quiet while his movement developed. Only a tiny group that became known as the Confessing Church resisted.

U.S. churches usually have found reason to support the nation's war efforts. In World War I, it was to make the world safe for democracy. In World War II, it was to oppose Hitler's awful regime. Perhaps the exception was Vietnam. Failure of the effort to stop communism aroused much church antiwar sentiment, which helped end the Vietnam War.

The causes always seemed good. In fact, however, despite the rare exception, churches have tended to have little understanding of the dynamics involved in causing the wars. Those dynamics had been put in motion and dictated by political, economic, and other forces animated by interests far from Christian. The churches did not understand these forces and had not bothered to try to understand them.

The sad fact, consequently, is that despite good intentions, the churches were agents of ethnocentrism. Both sides in nearly every war are convinced of the rightness of their cause. Typically, they claim the assistance of their deity.

This poses another challenge you should try to respond to creatively. It is a challenge to get and keep the members of your church interested in studying and trying to understand what is going on in international affairs. This important action should be added to your usual peace activities. Try to involve as many people as possible so there aren't just a few who are labeled disparagingly as "peaceniks."

Race Relations

Race relations have also been a concern to churches. Churches figured prominently in the 1960s civil rights struggle, which resulted in the integration of most public facilities. Church people, however, were not unanimous in support of the effort. Nor have they been in subsequent policy.

By and large, the church has been slower in accepting and practicing integration than most other institutions in society. It may still be true that it is the most segregated institution in our society.

Many denominations have managed fairly respectable, but still somewhat token, integration at the leadership levels. Integration in terms of membership of local churches, however, has been quite limited.

Effective programs in your church will need to continue to educate and persuade. God has "made of one blood all nations" (Acts 17:26, KJV). But many church members do not understand the fact. They need to be helped.

Serious study of what is meant by the term race is crucial for the church. Once it is begun, it will devolve quickly into a more modern and pertinent study of ethnic groups and interpersonal relations.

Past efforts toward racial integration were largely paternalistic, with white churches presuming that it was their prerogative to decide whether to accept blacks as members. That is not the way it works now. For true integration to occur, a basis of equality must be instituted: people must meet as equals and practice mutual respect.

This is the kind of integration you should seek. White churches will learn that it is not theirs to grant.

The best approach to improve relations between races in churches may be joint planning efforts and conducting activities that bring people together without implications of status. This can be for worship, fellowship, or Christian service.

Research has shown that prejudice is overcome best by bringing people together under conditions where it becomes more important not to hold prejudice than to hold it.

Capital Punishment

Taking of human life for any reason is abhorrent to many Christians. Consequently, some denominations have taken a stand against society's imposition of the death penalty for even the most serious crimes.

The rationale for this position is that capital punishment goes against the teachings of Jesus, that God's love and grace are extended to every person, that no sinner is beyond forgiveness and redemption, and that compounding evil by taking a life, usually for murder, makes society a murderer also.

The issue relates to the philosophy of punishment. Punishment can be for simple revenge, to deter the individual and others from the crime, to rehabilitate the individual, or to restore him or her to useful citizenship. Capital punishment is primarily a matter of revenge. It may have some minor deterring influence, but many studies have failed to verify this. Obviously, it makes rehabilitation impossible.

It is significant that in recent years the United States has reinstituted the practice of capital punishment. It had been banned for a time, as it still is in many other Western nations. Why the practice was restored in this country and is being used so extensively is a matter for serious consideration.

In addition to the restoration of capital punishment, the judicial system on the whole seems to be turning away from the objective of rehabilitation. Why this is so should be of serious concern to churches.

The great volume of serious crime is, unquestionably, a part of the reason. It could be, however, that something profoundly spiritual is happening to the American psyche. Are materialism, individualism, selfishness, and greed causing us to become callused and indifferent toward the worth of those who make trouble for us? The kind of alienation such an attitude implies seems a direct challenge to the Christian love ethic. Indifference toward it might indicate that the church is involved in the problem.

Only some local churches have developed deep interest in this matter. Most others, if interested at all, have focused on encouraging and helping those experiencing imprisonment or its aftermath. Church members or pastors visit incarceration centers, conduct worship services, establish interpersonal relationships, and sometimes help prisoners to adjust to life after prison when they are released. These are worthy ministries that should be encouraged, though they should be conducted with more care than they often receive.

I trust you will encourage the churches you serve to develop a broader understanding of the problem, and develop a program of action to embrace it more fully.

Counseling

Counseling usually is done with individuals, though to a limited extent, certain types of group counseling also are practiced. In either case, there are always social implications. Personal problems usually have social roots and need to be dealt with in terms of their social context.

More and more pastors are receiving seminary training in counseling. If you are fortunate to be one of them, you have learned that you should not try to function as a psychiatrist or psychologist, but as a pastor.

Many people in our high-pressure society are experiencing the need for counseling. Pastors are frequently the first ones they turn to. Often the pastor can give the kind of spiritual assistance needed and be a real help. It is important to be able to recognize other cases, however, where the problem is of a more complicated nature that requires the services of other professional specialists. In such cases, helping the client accept a carefully chosen referral qualifies as successful pastoral counseling.

Professional jealousy is unwise and unbecoming. You have no monopoly on helpful skills. Know your limits. One of the wisest things you can do is to locate ahead of time one or more good resources you can recommend with confidence. Consider psychiatrists, psychologists, medical doctors, family counselors, other pastors of more experience, social agencies, and other professionals according to resources available in your particular area. Do not select blindly. Try to make sure the referral resource functions in a manner compatible with your concerns as a minister.

Try to be the best counselor you can be, using what you know of the Bible and the spirit of Jesus. Combine this with what you have learned of psychology and what you can discover of social influences in the background of each case. Make referrals, when necessary, with reasoned care.

Be careful also in all other respects. Increasing alienation in society is encouraging legalism. Pastors are being sued for anything unwise they say or do in counseling.

Conclusion

The items on this list are not the only day-to-day concerns you may face, but they are among the most prominent ones that have received the attention of pastors and churches at various times and places. These issues will likely be among the first to require your attention.

Sensitivity to the requirement of social ministry may generate concerns of other kinds. Some of these are identified in the next chapter.

Chapter 10

Areas of Developing Crisis

Current trends suggest that humanity will face crises in several major areas in the not too distant future. Confrontation with most of them has already begun. Awareness of their seriousness, however, is still extremely limited, especially in the minds of pastors and churches. The need for Christian social action with respect to them is becoming increasingly evident.

The Population Explosion

It took until about A.D. 1500 for the human population to reach one billion. In the next three hundred years, the population doubled, and it reached three billion only a hundred years after that. We now number more than six billion, and every twelve years we add a billion more.

No one can be sure whether population growth will continue to surge, and the decline of growth in some industrialized nations suggest that global growth rates may eventually slow down. Other estimates suggest that in two hundred more years there could be an inconceivable fifty billion people.

Humanity faces a major decision. With faith in our God-given ability and responsibility, we can undertake to control our growth rate or we can maintain a laissez-faire attitude and leave the outcome to providence or chance.

Reliance on the laissez-faire attitude risks depending on population control by war, disease, or famine. It is another example of the perennial inclination to evade responsibility and try to maintain a position in which God can be blamed for the outcome.

In general, the church has been indifferent or only mildly interested in the problem. Where control has been proposed, the church has shown more opposition than willingness to sanction or participate.

Environmental Degradation

Another area of concern is the state of our physical environment, which is being polluted at an alarming rate. We are just beginning to realize that there is only a limited layer of air around our planet; that the water of rivers, lakes, and oceans can hold only a limited amount of poisons and debris and still remain viable; that forests can be reduced to a point where oxygen becomes dangerously scarce; and that valuable topsoil, vital to food production, can become so eroded and covered with concrete that it ceases to be available.

These are only a few of the alarming aspects of pollution. Most of them have begun to receive serious attention in little more than the last half century. Despite such efforts, pollution races far ahead of what is being accomplished to abate it.

Commitment to present practices makes the quality of the future very uncertain. Industries use chemicals to make products we think we can't do without, which results in huge quantities of poisonous waste. The use of nuclear power for weapons and electricity produces large quantities of dangerous waste that will not deteriorate for thousands of years. Unchecked use of coal and oil for fuel increasingly pollutes the air. Garbage and trash are piling up in such quantities that it is becoming difficult to find places to put it.

This doleful litany could go on and on. The voice of the church is exceedingly weak regarding environmental issues. Is there not more it can do than click its tongue and chant the word from Genesis about God giving humans dominion over the things of earth? There is a great need for the church to take its Bible-based convictions much more seriously.

The Revolution in Communication and Mobility

With only minor stretching of the facts, one can say that the twentieth century began without electricity, telephones, automobiles, radios, television, or airplanes. Today these items are so important to our daily existence that it now seems almost inconceivable that people could have lived without them. Yet they all have come on the scene in the span of one long lifetime.

As each new development occurred, it effected a radical change in life style. All of them, coming at almost the same time, produced an unprecedented revolution. Nearly every feature of existence, from eating habits to morals, was changed.

These amazing developments, however, were only a beginning. A flood of other innovations occurred in rapid succession: nuclear power, rockets, satellites, space exploration, computers, faxes, the Internet, and a host of other technological wonders.

As major as all of the changes have been, those related to transportation and communication have had the greatest significance for the church. Their impact is just beginning to be identified. Communications technology now allows every human impulse to be communicated instantly around the world. People are being more readily manipulated by propaganda. Cultures and their morals are in conflict. The world of human experience is shrinking to a single vast community.

Will understanding, appreciation, and love be communicated? Or will misunderstanding, ill will, and conflict be generated? Will all the ethnic groups, races, tribes, and nations be able to live together in a spirit of community?

These and a host of related matters constitute issues the church must stay aware of and do all it can to help guide developments.

The Economic System

As this text was being written, the United States Senate, composed principally of millionaires, voted down a bill that would have increased the minimum wage from $5.15 to $6.15 an hour. This means that some twelve million Americans will have to continue working for $2,900 less than the official poverty level for a family of three.

Today's economic system is based on power. It feeds impulses of greed and crushes the weak and helpless. The system makes little provision for the virtues of community and compassion, though it manages, in hobbled fashion, to provide for common need. Powerful individuals take advantage of the weak and often grow rich from their labors. Corporations pursue profit with little regard for the people who produce it. Powerful nations exploit and neglect the weak. The rich are a tiny minority in nearly every country, while a much larger proportion of the people live in abject, or near abject, poverty. Income levels in the most prosperous countries are many times what they are in the poorest countries.

Inequity, as it generally exists, prompted a spokesman from Denmark to speak with pride of his little country. It is so egalitarian, he said, that it has only about the same number of impoverished people as it has millionaires. Economic determinism is often cited as the ruling influence in human affairs. Certainly, economic interests have determined the course of history again and again.

Since the church is anchored to a gospel that says the love of money is the root of evil, it must maintain an ongoing quarrel with the economic system as it is currently operating. It must dare to criticize and suggest changes without letting itself be intimidated or bought off.

Economic greed and selfishness are alienating people from one another in every context around the world. They impede the expression of love and the realization of true community. Left in operation as the system presently permits, they portend increasing suffering and eventual disaster.

Alienation

As people are being brought closer together on a worldwide basis, two forces seem to be contesting for dominance of their relationships. One is the pull toward cooperation, community, and love. The other is the powerful inclination toward suspicion, hostility, and conflict. The church needs to be aware of the tension in this contest, and cast its influence as fully as possible on the side of community and love.

Alienation, resulting from the suspicion and hostility, is promoting the ultimate destruction of humanity. Short of that calamity, it is increasingly impeding the development of desperately needed community.

The growing tendency toward alienation, or treating one another callously, like strangers, is evident in countless ways. Lawyers and lawsuits proliferate. Social class divisions threaten to stifle democracy. Efficient distribution of wealth and goods to meet the needs of all is hampered by the greed of the most powerful. Ethnic groups, races, classes, and nationalities are finding it easier to develop prejudices, hide behind barricades, and engage in conflict with one another than to practice cooperation and community.

Like a root-rot, alienation threatens the flowering, indeed the very existence, of Christianity. It is an overt denial of the love and grace of God, a barrier to the flow of understanding, sympathy, and love between people.

Moral Decay

Radical social change, such as has occurred in this century, has a profound effect on many accepted ways of behaving. Introduction of the automobile, for example, changed courtship patterns because young people were enabled to escape supervision. Parents and neighborly gossip could no longer enforce the same boundaries.

Many similar changes have been underway in recent decades. Sometimes the changes are so many and are occurring so rapidly that they seem to be sweeping us along like an avalanche.

These effects on social change are already causing the church great anxiety, which is likely to increase in the future. This is because the church considers God to be the source of value, and is naturally concerned when values are at stake.

While God is, no doubt, the source of absolute value, the relative value structured in the society of a people may be only a dim understanding of the absolute. God gave humans valuing ability with the expectation that they would work to define the values by which they would live.

Because we need values to live by, all human groups define values designed to meet their needs. The definitions may be only approximations of what God had in mind to satisfy basic needs. Sometimes humans can misjudge their needs, or structure value definitions that have no relationship to basic, innate needs.

This means that there can be a measure of relativity in our morals as they have been defined. Social experience can change our understanding of need, resulting in a shift of the value perception. The social controls that protect the value then are shifted accordingly.

This kind of shift can occur without value loss. It may merely mean that values are in transition. The new way of behaving could be better than the old. At least, it probably will be better adapted to the changed circumstances.

Much of what is happening to morals at the present time, however, is of a different order. Modern means of mass communication, which can be and often is used under anonymous cover, have evolved so rapidly that effective social controls have not been developed for them. Consequently, ethics and morals are disregarded in the pursuit of profit, selfish interests, or propagandistic objectives. The result is increasing moral anarchy and ethical confusion, and indications are that it will become an ever more critical condition.

The church needs to understand both of these causes of moral change. What it can do about them is not clear, but it cannot afford to be indifferent. Appropriate action will require much prayer and creative effort.

Technology and Materialism

Technology has been a wonderful blessing to humanity, but not an unmitigated one. It is developing so rapidly that ethical definitions cannot keep up with it. Someone has said that humanity is running away with itself.

Technology has reduced the necessity of physical labor, but other kinds of tension-producing work have increased enormously. Employment opportunities have increased, but the market is becoming ever more elitist. Dislocations are occurring in the work force as jobs go to people with technical skills, putting the unskilled people at a disadvantage.

Many dangers exist in technological development that the church and all of humanity need to stay aware of. For example, the technical means of mass production may so outstrip development of the means for equitable distribution that great social unrest may occur.

As machines increasingly control the means of production, jobs for humans will decline and ownership and control may fall into fewer and fewer hands. The gap between rich and poor will probably grow wider and could perhaps even lead to new forms of oligarchy and serf-like dependency.

Technology is implicated in environmental damage. It is contributing to denigration of physical labor. It risks subjecting the human organism to excessive strain and tension.

The greatest hazard of all, perhaps, is the possibility that technology will so dominate human activity that it will cause the loss of many other important interests and values. For example, technical interests are dominating education to the detriment of studies in the arts, letters, philosophy, and social sciences. Even interest in religion is being seriously eroded by the fascination and obsession with the machines and gadgetry produced by technology, and by the work styles and recreational interests that technology spawns.

Pressure to Unify

Pressure toward integration and unification is developing on many fronts, mainly because technology has brought us all together and made us interdependent, also because we as a species are becoming more mature and sensitive.

Countries are finding it expedient or necessary to form larger units for trade, joint ventures, and mutual protection. The United Nations, NATO, international economic organizations, and ventures like the space station are examples of these large, cooperative units.

Europe is moving toward being a single economic unit, with one currency. International corporations are springing up rapidly and international organizations are being established. Knowledge, styles, and other aspects of culture are being shared.

Despite reluctance, protests, and resistance, the world is moving rapidly toward becoming a single social unit. Under pressure from global capitalism, some cultures are at risk of losing their unique features.

The division of the world into a multiplicity of political units—nations—is proving to be a clumsy, inefficient arrangement. Sooner or later, nations as they are presently known will probably lose autonomy and independence.

Religious bodies are becoming increasingly ecumenical. A World Council of Churches has been organized. To encourage inter-religious dialogue, a twelfth International Meeting of People and Religions brought together Muslims, Catholics, Orthodox, Protestant, Jewish, and other religious groups in Bucharest, Romania, in August 1998.

Crises of many kinds will be generated as this unifying process continues. It will be important for the church to remain aware of what is taking place and why. The church will have to decide whether to serve as interpreter, advocate, or opponent of events as they occur.

Conclusion

This is by no means a complete list of areas in which crises are developing. These eight are ones in which the major trends are highly visible, but there are many others of significant dimensions.

A revolution is underway. Few aspects of culture and social organization are unaffected. The church cannot be a spectator, sitting on the sidelines; it must join the the action. As the living body of Christ, it cannot be apathetic where the needs of the poor, the sick, the neglected, the imprisoned, the mistreated, or any other of God's children cry out for its assistance. The changes that are underway are already proving to be painful and costly, and could become more so.

Chapter 11

Theological Considerations

My training is as a social scientist, rather than as a theologian or philosopher. Nevertheless, I would like to draw on my experience as a pastor and teacher, including twenty years on the faculty of a theological seminary, to raise a few questions that will have a bearing on how you view social action as part of your ministerial responsibility.

The primary question is this: How serious are we both about representing the spirit of Jesus and the hopes of the kingdom of God on earth?

Let us begin with your worldview. Is it static or dynamic? Of course, it can be a mixture of both, but you probably are more inclined to one direction than the other.

A static view sees God as having made the world and all things in it, fixed its laws, principles, and values, and then backed away to watch it operate. His judgment would be passed on humans in terms of how well they conformed to his fixed laws. His church would be an established entity, a kind of fixed portal into heaven and eternity.

A dynamic view sees God involved in his creation, particípating in the process of its functioning. In this mode, he would be interacting with his human offspring, assisting them with their problems, encouraging them toward fulfillment of their potential, and judging them only as they err and shut him out. The church would be a continuation of the incarnation in Jesus, a living, growing, vital presence and an expression of the prayer "thy kingdom come, thy will be done, on earth as it is in heaven (Matt. 6:10)."

This dynamic view gives me a warm feeling of fellowship and partnership with God. It gives me hope that there is redeeming purpose in the universe and in my personal existence. It keeps me struggling toward the ideal that Jesus set before me, the ideal of God's will being done on earth, and of my becoming increasingly mature in Christ.

Closely related to this general worldview is the personal view of how you think of God and his action. Do you think of him primarily as having acted in the past, and having spoken his absolute final word? Or do you think of him as being as alive and active today as he has ever been? Did he once speak to human minds and hearts in ways he no longer practices? And has he already done the valuing that humans have to struggle with? Or does he engage with them in the valuing process?

To me, God is as much alive today as he has ever been. I think of him as speaking to human minds and hearts in the same ways in which he has always spoken: he helps us think his thoughts, and value as he values. Our finitude, immaturity, and the sin of estrangement from him, it seems to me, keep us from understanding him perfectly.

How do you think God feels about the world of human society and culture? Does he see it as a man-made product, full of sin and evil? As a briar patch from which only those who throw themselves completely on his mercy and grace will be rescued to a better life hereafter? Or can you think of God loving the world, interacting with people in their culture-building process and seeing the process as a garden for the cultivation of eternal quality in their lives?

God's judgment has to function, of course. Yet I believe that God did not give creative powers to humans just so he could condemn them for trying to use those powers. I think of him as interacting with us as we structure our world, guiding us when we will let him, judging and correcting us when we make mistakes, and helping us when our movement is toward his kingdom here on earth.

This leads to the question of how you feel about the purpose of life here on earth. Is it a curse to be born? Do we merely experience a time and place of trial and tribulation, from which we must try to merit being rescued by God's grace? Or does God want us to exult in life, to rejoice in the privilege, and to let him guide us in the ways of life eternal?

Needless to say, I think of this life and of this world as basically good, despite the troubles and trials we all experience. It is the focus of my conscious experience; I have no desire to escape. I trust God, who created me, for whatever the future may hold for me. This life is the arena of privilege where I may discover, if I will, the meanings that comprise the quality that eternal life should have.

How do you view the Bible? Do you see it as literally dictated by God, and therefore absolutely true in every jot and tittle? If not, in what other sense is it God's word, and true? Is it God's only, or final, word? I have found such questions extremely puzzling, though I grew up believing the Bible came down directly from heaven, printed in the King James Version and with a black leather binding.

Arguments over Scripture's literal and absolute truth, it seems to me, only confuse and mislead. Such debates make it difficult to understand the Bible and to appreciate the God so wonderfully revealed in it. To me, the Bible seems much more understandable as an inspired, but humanly produced document, telling of a sensitive and thoughtful people's responsive relationship to a self-revealing God. This interactive relationship occurred through a long and trying history, and people's understanding only slowly increased.

Eventually, on the basis of their partial understanding, God revealed himself in human form as one of their own . In this form, God indicated what human life could and should be. He revealed his plan for the salvation of all people.

The church, which was established on the basis of the revelation in Jesus, is charged with the responsibility to continue that revelation. God is still alive. He still loves his human creations. He is still laboring with them to create the kind of world he wants them to have.

God still speaks to human hearts. His redeeming purpose continues. He seeks the fellowship of understanding, responsive love. His will is to see his kingdom increasingly come through his free but committed human offspring.

Finally, how do you feel about the present state of the church? Should it concern itself about conditions in society?

My understanding is that, as the Bible indicates, the church is the body of Christ, still alive in the world to continue his redemptive mission, still alive to keep the world reminded of God's love. This is the spiritual essence of its reality. As a social reality, however, it is an institution, what Max Weber might have called "a routinization of charisma."

Jesus' followers wanted to preserve and pass on to others the meaning of their experience with him. The disciples formed a nucleus around which the organization took shape. Rituals and routines at their meetings were based on things Jesus had said and done. For a time, the memory of him was almost as real as his presence had been.

Gradually the routines became fixed and more elaborate. Effort was required to keep them alive and meaningful, and keeping the momentum in the organization became important. The church as an institution was created, and became the focus of attention with its institutional requirements competing with the memory of Jesus and his message.

Through the ages, the church has experienced the tension caused by this competition. At its best, the church has been an earthen vessel carrying, sharing, and proclaiming the good news of Jesus. There have been times, however, when its institutional requirements have overshadowed, even seemed to eclipse, the purpose for which the institution was formed. This has amounted to a form of idolatry.

Church history is replete with efforts to call the church back from its institutional self-concern to the purpose it was created for. Monasticism was such an effort, as was the Protestant Reformation.

The paramount question for us today should be this: Have we let institutional interests take precedence over the gospel's message and purpose? Much evidence indicates that we have.

We quibble endlessly over points of doctrine. Our denominations often compete rather than cooperate. We give major attention to buildings, budgets, liturgical procedures, rules, and regulations. We take great care to protect and preserve the church's reputation and social image, even at the cost of muting the message of God's judgment and love.

Where is the self-sacrificing spirit of Jesus on his way to the cross? Where is the message of God's unlimited love for the world? Where is the prayer really being said for the kingdom of God to come on earth? Where is the spirit that prompted early Christians to go to the stake, the Roman arena, and other sacrificial places to set the world on fire with the good news of the gospel?

Your answers to questions such as these will determine whether you see social action as a vital part of the church's

agenda. Such questions could make you uncomfortable with
the idea of operating the church as a nursery for immature
souls waiting for transport to heaven. Hopefully they will
inspire you to be a part of God's purpose to transform and
redeem the world of human society, to see evil defeated and
eliminated from its social structures and practices, to see
alienation replaced by a spirit of community and love, and
to see soul-crushing perversity and neglect changed to
wholesome and nurturing influences. Indeed, honest answers
to such basic questions would hopefully fill you with passion
to lead the church out of its comfortable doldrums into an
active program of obedience to God's loving purpose for the
salvation of his children in their imperfect world.

Societies and cultures, like individuals, must be con-
verted. What we call the ethos, or spirit, is to a culture much
the same as the soul is to the person. It needs redemption by
the grace of God and change in its physical forms and structures. This is a dimension of evangelism to which the church
is being challenged. It may be the next giant step in God's
revelation of his redeeming purpose.

It must surely be to this task of redeeming society that
you have been called. It is not a separate part of your calling, but rather an integral part of the whole. Society cannot
be redeemed without redeemed people in it. God wants you
to help win the souls of alienated individuals. He wants you
to help those individuals enter into the joy-filled meanings
of eternal life. He wants you to inspire them and help them
in their responsibility as transformers of the society where
the souls of his children are nurtured.

To see your calling in this wholistic sense should be no
reason for discouragement. The task is large, yet it is privileged work in the heart of God's purpose. He promises to
be with you in full partnership.

Chapter 12

The Urgent Imperative

God challenges human beings to take responsibility for their world. He wants us to overcome our selfishness and become mature beings. While he does not abandon us to our difficult tasks, the Creator does refuse to do our work for us. He does not guarantee our success, though he assures us that he will be with us, help us, and pursue his purpose beyond our personal efforts.

God's challenge is seen in the marvelous abilities and insights he has helped humans acquire. He has shown us that we are not as helpless and dependent as we have always assumed we are. God is warning us with evidence of the risks we are taking with irresponsible use of our abilities. He is trying to make us see the potentiality in the opportunities he is presenting us, potentiality for joining with him in structuring his kingdom on earth.

The possibilities are infinite, and the situation is urgent. To be convinced of this requires only an informed look at how some of the everyday facts we live with have stifled our awareness:

- Technology that produces long-range rockets and nuclear bombs can cause—at a moment's notice—worldwide mass destruction, when the technology is in the hands of war-spirited political entities.

- The population explosion is threatening to overwhelm the earth's limited resources and human skills of organization.
- The physical environment is becoming dangerously polluted.
- Crude social arrangements are creating extreme disparities and inequities, which people cannot be expected to endure indefinitely.
- The disjointed world of ethnicity, race, and tribalism is being thrown together in a single megalopolis, with a threat of chaos and self-destruction.

Like boils on the body, these afflictions which have been building in the social system through the ages, have, in the last few decades, suddenly come to a life-threatening stage. The condition should not be taken lightly, nor viewed with complacency.

The church understands itself to be God's special instrument for the expression of his love for the world. It is uniquely positioned and equipped for the saving task his love purposes. But will it perform as it needs to perform?

You and the congregations you serve will be part of the answer. The church that Margaret Mead called "the dullest old thing still around" certainly will not be what God wants or needs. The church that comforts, but does not challenge, cannot succeed. A church that preaches pessimism about the human world and encourages escapist attitudes in Jesus' followers will never even sense the challenge.

Is there no doubt that it was for times such as these that God brought the church into the world? The church has remarkable strengths: human and financial resources, a worldwide presence, an increasing spirit of inclusiveness, and a growing understanding of the universe and of God's purpose for it. The simple mysticism the church (and the rest of the human race) started with has been replaced with a more profound and mature mysticism, one that is informed by science and a more realistic appraisal of reality.

The church is uniquely positioned and equipped to be God's special agent of redemption in a confused, lost world. It needs to be awakened to a fresh, enlarged vision of its responsibility.

Your role as a church leader is to help bring God's people back to their biblical heritage of concern for others and for the world. In the Old Testament, faith was essentially a social experience. In the New Testament, Christianity became a religion for the whole world, and faith in Jesus began to be understood as a prayer for the coming of God's kingdom on earth.

For a time, this social awareness was obscured. Joyful awareness of God's saving grace for individuals, which was so explicit and easily understood in the ministry of Jesus, absorbed the church's initial interest.

Now the whole thrust of the gospel has become evident. The church, however, which had oriented itself so completely to the salvation, care, and nurturing of individual souls, is having difficulty reorienting itself to this larger understanding of its responsibility.

Assimilating this larger understanding, however, is essential to the church's survival today. It is also the best hope for the survival of humanity. As Paul said, "While God has overlooked the times of human ignorance, now he commands all people everywhere to repent" (Acts 17:30).

The church will likely survive as an institution as long as humans survive. It will continue going through its cycle, becoming established but so secularized that it will have little non-social meaning. It will be reborn as a movement focused on simple mysticism, and move gradually again into status, secularization, and the necessity of another rebirth.[32]

The redemptive influence that God requires for the salvation of the world, however, will not be operative in it. The church will have become a part of the world needing salvation. Previous revelations indicate that this would not be the agenda God wants for the church. He is still in the process of building the church into the structure he wants it to be.

You are, I think, among those whom God is calling to help his church awaken to its larger responsibility. God knows the responsibility is great, and the task will be hard. But can you be pleased with yourself if you pervert your calling into a life of comfortable complacency, as keeper of a sheepfold, or a nursery?

The discouragements may be many, but they will not come close to the suffering of Jesus on the cross. Faith in God and in the importance of the task will sustain you.

Admittedly, the saving of the world is too big an undertaking for you. It will not be accomplished in your lifetime. You will labor to exhaustion and will seem hardly to have made a dent in the problem. The results will have to be left in God's hands. He will know how to make it work together with the good in other lives to produce the ends he desires.

I have urged you to make social action a conscious dimension of your ministry. My hope is that it will be a sensible, positive thrust in all you do as a pastor; that you will help the congregations you serve to grow in their understanding and vision of what the church can and should be.

I am reminded of a popular club in a senior citizens' organization. Its title is "The Never Give Up Club." Christians are infused with the optimism of faith. They never give up because they know God does not give up.

Do's and Don'ts

Since I have tried to make this a direct and personal message, let me conclude with a few personal admonitions. You may call them some Do's and Don'ts, noted with deep concern for you.

Do's

- Communicate fully, openly, and sincerely with the people of your congregation.
- Trust your people to understand; be open and above board with them.
- Approach them always in the strength and conviction of meekness.
- Share with them as fully as possible the insights and understandings you have concerning social issues and the bearing of Scripture on social issues.
- Recognize the limitations of your knowledge and understanding.
- Be willing to learn from your lay people. They have been out in the world and have much knowledge to share.
- Keep lay people in the lead at every possible point in the social ministry of the congregation.

Don'ts

- Don't try to do everything, especially at the same time. There is a world of problems, and your resources are limited. Choose what seems most relevant, urgent, and possible with available resources (remembering always the range of faith).
- Never try to drive people. Instead, persuade, challenge, lead, and share with them.
- Don't be egotistical, pretending to know it all. If you have prophetic insight, share it with conviction, but recognize the right of others to question or disagree.
- Don't be distraught or discouraged when lay people disagree with you. Try to understand their views and make

sure they understand yours. If you are sure of your position, hold to it, but respect them in their right to disagree.

God bless you in your ministry. Rightly seen, it is the most important work in the world.

Notes

1. Walter Rauschenbusch, *A Theology of the Social Gospel* (Nashville: Abingdon Press, undated), Apex series, paperback.

2. *Religion in the News,* 1:1 (June 1998), Center for the Study of Religion in Public Life, Trinity College, Hartford, Conn.

3. *Encyclopedia Britannica,* 1962 ed., s.v. "preaching."

4. Robert H. Bonthius, "Pastoral Care for Structures—As Well as Persons," in *Pastoral Care,* May 1967.

5. Rauschenbusch, *A Theology of the Social Gospel,* as quoted in John Dillenberger and Claude Welch, *Protestant Christianity* (New York: Charles Scribner's Sons, 1955), p. 248.

6. Dieter T. Hessel, ed., *Theological Education and Social Ministry* (New York: The Pilgrim Press, 1988), p. 2.

7. Martin Luther King, Jr., *Letters from a Birmingham Jail* as quoted in Hessel, 2nd ed., *Social Ministry* (Louisville: Westminster/John Knox Press, 1992), p. 9.

8. Carl S. Dudley, *Next Steps in Community Ministry* (Alban Institute Publication, 1996), p. 9.

9. *Ibid.,* xii.

10. *Ibid.,* p. xiii.

11. John H. Yoder, *The Politics of Jesus* (Grand Rapids, Mich.: Wm. B. Eerdmans Publishing Co., 1972), p. 27.

12. Gustavo Gutierrez, *A Theology of Liberation: History, Politics and Salvation* (Maryknoll, N.Y.: Orbis, 1971).

13. Bruce D. Rahtjen, *Scripture and Social Action*

(Nashville: Abingdon, 1966), pp. 100-104.

14. May-June issue, 1998, p. 3.

15. Quoted in Hessel, *Social Ministry,* rev. ed., (Louisville, Ky.: Westminster/John Knox Press, 1992), p. 95.

16. Hessel, ed., *Theological Education*, p. 116.

17. Alan Jones, executive director, San Francisco United Methodist Mission. As quoted in *Newscope,* Vol. 26, No. 39/September 25, 1998. Again, some of these actions—such as inviting candidates to speak in the worship service—should be approached with great care.

18. As quoted in Hessel, *Theological Education*, p. 12.

19. Dudley, p. 21.

20. Frank Chikane, *No Life of My Own* (Maryknoll, N. Y.: Orbis, 1989), p. 45.

21. James H. Cone, *Speaking the Truth: Ecumenism, Liberation, and Black Theology* (Grand Rapids, Mich.: Wm. B. Eerdmans Publishing Co, 1981) p.118.

22. As quoted in James Melvin Washington, ed., *A Testimony of Hope: The Essential Writings of Martin Luther King, Jr.* (San Francisco: Harper & Row, 1986), p. 299.

23. Hessel, Dieter T., *Social Ministry*, rev. ed. (Louisville, Ky.: Westminster/John Knox Press, 1992), pp. 121- 123.

24. Edgar R. Trexler, ed., *Creative Congregations: Tested Strategies for Today's Churches* (Nashville, Tenn.: Abingdon, 1972), pp. 65-68.

25. Taylor Branch, *Parting the Waters: America in the King Years, 1954-1963* (New York: Simon & Schuster, 1988), pp. 115-6.

26. Harvey Seifert, *The Church in Community Action* (New York: Abingdon-Cokesbury, Press, 1952), p. 99.

27. Based on "A Force for Every Task," by Donald L. Collins in Trexler. ed., *Creative Congregations: Tested Strategies for Today's Churches* (Nashville, Tenn.: Abingdon, 1972), pp. 17-24.

28. Hessel, *Social Ministry*, p.146.

29. H. Richard Niebuhr, *The Purpose of the Church and Its Ministry* (New York: Harper & Brothers, 1956).

30 Peter Andrew Wells, *Thou Shalt: Social Justice Ministry in Small Church Settings*, Project Thesis, Wesley Theological Seminary, Washington, D. C., 1996.

31. Haskell M. Miller, *Understanding and Preventing Juvenile Delinquency* (Nashville, Tenn.: Abingdon, 1958).

32. Rodney Stark and William Sims Bainbridge, *The Future of Religion: Secularization, Revival, and Cult Formation* (Berkeley: University of California Press, 1985).

Select Bibliography

Bennett, John C. *When Christians Make Political Decisions.* New York: Association Press, 1964.

Berton, Pierre. *The Comfortable Pew.* Philadelphia: Lippincott, 1965.

Carlson-Thies, Stanley W., and James W. Skillen, eds. *Welfare in America: Christian Perspectives On a Policy in Crisis.* Grand Rapids, Mich.: Wm. B. Eerdmans Publishing Co., 1996.

Chikane, Frank. *No Life of My Own.* Maryknoll, N. Y.: Orbis, 1989.

Cone, James H. *Speaking the Truth: Ecumenism, Lberation, and Black Theology.* Grand Rapids, Mich.: Wm. B. Eerdmans Publishing Co., 1981.

Curran, Charles E. *History and Contemporary Issues: Studies in Moral Theology.* New York: Continuum, 1996.

Dudley, Carl S. *Next Steps in Community Ministry: Hands-on Leadership.* Bethesda, Md.: Alban Institute Publications, 1996.

Gardiner, Clinton. *Biblical Faith and Social Ethics.* New York: Harper, 1960.

Gutierrez, Gustavo. *A Theology of Liberation: History, Politics and Salvation.* Maryknoll, N.Y.: Orbis, 1971.

Gunderson, Gary. *Deeply Woven Roots: Improving the Quality of Life in Your Community.* Minneapolis, Minn.: Fortress Press, 1997.

Hessel, Dieter T. *Social Ministry*. Revised Edition. Louisville, Ky.: Westminster/John Knox Press, 1992.

Hessel, Dieter T., ed. *Theological Education for Social Ministry*. New York: The Pilgrim Press, 1988.

Hinsdale, Mary Ann, Helen Matthews Lewis, and S. Maxine Waller. *Community Development and Local Theology*. Philadelphia: Temple University Press, 1995.

Holland, Joe, and Peter Hanriot, S. J. *Social Analysis: Linking Faith and Justice*. Washington, D. C.: Center of Concern, 1980.

Leas, Speed, and Paul Kittlaus. *The Pastoral Counselor in Social Action*. Philadelphia: Fortress Press, 1981.

Miller, Haskell M. *Understanding and Preventing Juvenile Delinquency*. Nashville, Tenn.: Abingdon Press, 1958.

Miller, Kenneth R., and Mary Elizabeth Wilson. *The Church That Cares: Identifying and Responding to Needs in Your Community*. Valley Forge, Pa.: Judson Press, 1985.

Niebuhr, H. Richard. *The Purpose of the Church and Its Ministry*. New York: Harper & Brothers, 1956.

Rahtgen, Bruce D. *Scripture and Social Action*. Nashville, Tenn.: Abingdon Press, 1966.

Rauschenbusch, Walter. *A Theology of the Social Gospel*. Nashville, Tenn.: Abingdon Press, Apex series, paperback, undated.

Seifert, Harvey. *The Church in Community Action*. New York: Abingdon-Cokesbury Press, 1952.

Schweitzer, Albert. *The Quest for the Historical Jesus*. New York: Macmillan, paperback, n.d. (Original English trans. 1910).

Trexler, R. Edgar, ed. *Creative Congregations: Tested Strategies for Today's Churches.* Nashville, Tenn.: Abingdon Press, 1972.

Washington, James Melvin, ed. *A Testimony of Hope: The Essential Writings of Martin Luther King, Jr.* San Francisco: Harper & Row, 1986.

Wells, Peter Andrew. "Thou Shalt: Justice Ministry in Small Church Settings." Thesis, Wesley Theological Seminary, Washington, D. C, 1996.

Winter, Gibson. *America in Search of Its Soul.* Harrisburg, Pa: Morehouse, 1996.

Wogaman, J. Philip. *Speaking the Truth in Love: Prophetic Preaching to a Broken World.* Louisville: Westminster/John Knox, 1998.

Yoder, John H. *The Politics of Jesus.* Grand Rapids, Mich.: Wm. B. Eerdmans Publishing Co, 1972.

The Author

Haskell M. Miller is Professor Emeritus of Sociology and Social Ethics, Wesley Theological Seminary, Washington, D.C. He is a minister of the United Methodist Church with more than fifty years experience, half in the pastorate and half in college, university, and seminary settings.

A native of Texas and a graduate of Southern Methodist University (Dallas), Miller also has a Ph.D. from New York University.